IOWA
A Taste of Home

Cover Photo:
A Hat Full of Morels
by Jodi Bellmann
Dubuque

Jodi Bellmann, a Dubuque County 4-H'er, discovered a nice patch of morel mushrooms in the woods near her home. "Because morels are a tasty treat, they can be used to make many different things," said Jodi. A member of the Peru Achievers 4-H Club, Jodi has been enrolled in photography for four years. Jodi's parents are Dennis and Terry Bellmann.

Iowa: A Taste of Home

To 4-H Families and Friends

We are excited to present to you our second statewide 4-H cookbook, *Iowa: A Taste of Home*. It is a sequel to our first cookbook, *Coming Home to Iowa*, which was published in 1992. The tremendous success of that publication prompted us to again search the state for a new generation of kitchen classics.

We specifically asked Iowa 4-H members to share with us a favorite dish from their family. The response was great! We received hundreds of recipes. Some have been passed down through the generations, others are original creations; but all of the recipes are special to these young people.

A big **Thank You** goes to everyone who submitted a recipe or photograph. We regret that all of them could not be published. All entries were initially sorted by the cookbook committee, but the staff of Favorite Recipes® Press made the final selection.

It takes the work of many people to make a project like this successful. Special thanks go to our 4-H club volunteers, county Extension staff, and the trustees of the Iowa 4-H Foundation for their cooperation.

Finally, we would like to thank you for supporting this fund-raising project. The proceeds earned from cookbook sales will help the Iowa 4-H Foundation continue its mission "to assist Iowa's youth in becoming productive, self-directed, contributing members of society."

Cookbook Committee

Patti Blum, Harlan
Katie Bogue, Ogden
Bev Carstensen, Maxwell

Albert Grunenwald, Ames
Chad Harris, Shenandoah
Angela Pithan, Anthon

Kevin Roberts, Conroy
Marian Storjohann, Davenport

Special Assistance

Patricia Anderson
Florine M. Swanson

Iowa 4-H Foundation
Marketing Committee

Solutions, Incorporated
Des Moines

Iowa State University, the Iowa 4-H Foundation, and Favorite Recipes® Press (an imprint of FRP™) are not responsible for the nutritional profiles provided at the end of each recipe if ingredients are substituted. Nor can they be held responsible for any product listed in this book. The recipes are home-tested and are not endorsed by Iowa State University or the Iowa 4-H Foundation. This cookbook is a collection of our favorite recipes and are not necessarily original recipes.

Published by FRP™
P.O. Box 305142, Nashville, Tennessee 37230
1-800-358-0560

Copyright© Iowa 4-H Foundation
32 Curtiss Hall, ISU • Ames, Iowa 50011
(515) 294-1537

Library of Congress: 97-72385
ISBN: 0-9657893-0-6

Manufactured in the United States of America
First Printing: 1997 12,500 copies

Iowa: A Taste of Home

Table of Contents

A Taste of 4-H History 4
Lois Edmonds' First Place Bread Recipe 5
A Taste of 4-H in 1924 6
A Taste of 4-H Today 7
Nutritional Profile Guidelines 8
Appetizers, Snacks, and Beverages 9
Soups and Salads 27
Breads 45
Vegetables, Side Dishes, and Accompaniments 63
Holidays and Special Occasions 81
Main Dishes 99
Bars and Cookies 125
Cakes, Pies, and Desserts 143
What's the Best Nutrition Advice? 163
Food Guide Pyramid 164
Making the Pyramid Work 165
What Is a Serving? 166
Index 167
Give a Gift That Says "Thank You!" 171
The Great 4-H Alumni Search 173
Order Information 175

❖ Low-Fat Recipes (30% or less calories from fat and
215 or less total calories per serving)

A Taste of 4-H History

Iowa 4-H and food have a longstanding tradition. Before the days of head, heart, hands, and health, there were agriculture clubs for boys and home culture clubs for girls. It was Cap E. Miller, superintendent of Keokuk County schools, who in 1904 first organized these clubs for Iowa boys and girls. In 1906, O. H. Benson, superintendent of Wright County schools, introduced elementary agriculture and domestic science courses into the regular classwork. Benson gave examinations and school credit for the work. Yet another school superintendent in Page county, Jessie Field, is credited for further developing club projects. In 1908, her girls' program included baking, sewing, patching, darning, and basketry.

The remarkable work of these early school superintendents was stimulated by help from Iowa State College. The college Extension Service sponsored state contests in corn, oats, potato and garden growing, cooking, sewing, and home management. It was at the first state baking contest in 1911 where twelve-year-old Lois Edmonds baked the champion loaf of bread. Edmonds, a Page County school girl, earned a trip to Washington, D.C. with her mother. There they were received by President Taft and the Secretary of Agriculture, "Tama Jim" Wilson.

Jessie Field wrote about Lois Edmonds in a 1912 article for a YWCA publication. Field indicated that Edmonds was "not the least spoiled by her victory." Field described her as "a sweet, modest, wholesome little girl . . . always ready to put the happiness of others before her own." The only thing that changed about Edmonds was her baking flour. Ira Shambaugh donated *Shambaugh's Sweet and Pure Flour* to the country school kids who were preparing for the state contest. When Edmonds won the contest, the mill changed the name of the flour to *Shambaugh's Prize*.

There is one more note of historical interest to the bread baking story. The working relationship between Ira Shambaugh and the school superintendent, Jessie Field, turned to a romantic one. When Jessie returned to Clarinda, after five years serving the YWCA in New York City, she was met by Ira and a spontaneous group of local "Y" girls. The girls were heard chanting, "He comes to the station to meet his relation, for **she's** Shambaugh's prize." The couple married in 1917.

Sources Cited:
Field, Jessie, "A Country Girl I Know," *YWCA Association Monthly*, Sept. 1912.
  Reck, Franklin M., *The 4-H Story*, 1951.

Special Thanks to Ruth Shambaugh Watkins for providing additional background information about her parents, Ira and Jessie, and for Lois Edmonds' award winning recipe.

Lois Edmonds'
First Place Bread Recipe

(As written in a letter to her aunt around 1912)

2 cups scalded milk (whole milk)
3 tablespoons sugar
2 tablespoons salt (scant)
2 tablespoons butter (generous)
$1/2$ cake compressed yeast
4 cups flour (about)

Put sugar, salt and butter in bread bowl. Pour over the scalded milk. When cooled to 100 degrees F. take 2 tablespoons of this mixture and add the yeast. Work until smooth in a cup. Then add to the bowl of liquid stirring well with wooden spoon. Begin adding the sifted flour beating thoroughly. When dough becomes too stiff to handle with spoon, turn it on floured board and work with hands, kneading in more flour as dough becomes sticky. Knead the dough until it becomes soft, smooth, and elastic. This is when the yeast and air bubbles are distributed evenly through the mass. Continue kneading about one hour.

Grease a warmed bowl. Invert the dough in bowl, then turn over and cover closely with a warmed cloth. Set to rise in a pan of water the temperature of which is 110 degrees F. Temperature of room should be about 70 degrees F. When the dough has doubled in size turn out on board, knead lightly about five or ten minutes. Then return to bowl for final rising; when it comes up again turn out, divide in loaves, work lightly pressing down evenly all around and put in pans. You can set to rise over the warm water, cover closely and when double in bulk put in an oven which will brown a piece of paper in eight or ten minutes. Bake 50 minutes. The last 15 minutes should be slightly cooler than the first 15.

This should make two loaves about 4x5x10 inches. Bake an even brown all over. Stand to cool in air, uncovered. Do not use too much flour.

Lois Edmonds,
Clarinda,
Page County, Iowa

A Taste of 4-H in 1924

4-H Club Refreshments by Florence Packman

(Taken from an Iowa Extension Home Economics Bulletin, July 1924)

What shall we serve? This is an easy question with an equally easy answer, if we as Club Girls will only make it so.

First of all, the charm of our refreshments lies largely in their simplicity. Gone are the days when we spent a large part of 24 hours painstakingly hollowing our orange baskets and laboriously decorating them till they resembled curiosities rather than something good to eat. This does not mean that our refreshments should not be attractive; rather it means the opposite. But it does mean that our refreshments must be easy to prepare and limited in number. A good rule followed in many clubs is: "Serve not more than two foods."

Secondly, let us remember that refreshments served at club meetings are to promote sociability rather than to supply one of the three daily meals. Whatever we serve should be light and dainty, pleasing to the eye, and appetizing in flavor. The food served should not be expensive nor should it require too much time in preparation. And let's remember that our mother's place is in the living room with the club members, not in the kitchen fussing with salads and cakes. Courtesy, like charity, begins at home—with thoughtfulness for our mother. Some clubs have made it a rule that the refreshments must be prepared by the members themselves.

Summer Refreshments

Perhaps you are to have the Garner Township Clothing Club at your home in July. If so, your refreshments will of course be decidedly different than when you entertain them the following January.

When the mercury climbs to the very tip of the thermometer, wouldn't you like to serve your favorite salad, or a cold refreshing drink of some kind? On a sultry summer day the food must be tart enough and icy cold.

If you have stirred and stewed over a hot stove all morning, your spirits will wilt along with your starchy gingham apron. A lot of fussing in the kitchen is bound to conflict with hospitality. Let's remember always to greet our guests enthusiastically. Even the most piping-hot food on earth would not be enjoyed if you had given your friends a lukewarm welcome. After a long, hard morning in the kitchen the most gracious of hostesses would be so tired that the club meeting would prove anything but the recreation it should be.

Four-H Special

2 cups cooked green beans, cut in small pieces
1 cup chopped celery
2 teaspoons chopped onion

Mix the above ingredients, combine with salad dressing, arrange on crisp lettuce leaves, and sprinkle on top with grated cheese.

A Taste of 4-H Today

The Iowa 4-H program is built on Iowa traditions of strong family, education, and rural heritage. Today more than 100,000 Iowa youth experience the Youth and 4-H program through community clubs, special interest groups, or school enrichment programs. The program strives to reach youth in town and urban settings as well as those in rural parts of the state.

An important strength of the Iowa 4-H program is the intergenerational learning that occurs when adults and young people work together. Adult mentors help 4-H members discover their own potential through project work, community service, and leadership opportunities. Alumni often credit the 4-H program with the communication, leadership, and record keeping skills they now use in their careers. Former 4-H'ers are active in their communities and take pride in serving as volunteers.

Today's Youth and 4-H program is reaching out to high risk youth whether they are rural or urban. Programs in science and biotechnology, agriculture and natural resources, work force preparation, and community service are just a few of the ways we are reaching new audiences. We have also expanded the program to include kids in grades K-3. The Iowa 4-H Foundation has supported this initiative by funding two program assistants. The assistants are developing Clover Kid programs in 17 Iowa counties.

Annually, the Iowa 4-H Foundation provides over $350,000 in educational program grants, financial assistance for youth and volunteers, recognition awards and scholarships, and facility maintenance for the Iowa 4-H Education and Natural Resources Center. These dollars help us to address the issues that will continue to challenge youth in the future.

Iowa: A Taste of Home provides the opportunity for the extended 4-H family to share some of its favorite traditions with you. The proceeds will continue the work of the Iowa 4-H Foundation to make a positive difference in the lives of young Iowans.

I hope you enjoy trying the recipes in this cookbook knowing the wonderful gift you have provided to 4-H.

Sincerely,

Joseph R. Kurth
Director of Youth and 4-H Programs

Nutritional Profile Guidelines

The editors have attempted to present these family recipes in a format that allows approximate nutritional values to be computed. Persons with dietary or health problems or whose diets require close monitoring should not rely solely on the nutritional information provided. They should consult their physicians or a registered dietitian for specific information.

Abbreviations for Nutritional Profile

Cal — Calories	Sod — Sodium	Prot — Protein
T Fat — Total Fat	Carbo — Carbohydrates	g — grams
Chol — Cholesterol	Fiber — Dietary Fiber	mg — milligrams

Nutritional information for these recipes is computed from information derived from many sources, including materials supplied by the United States Department of Agriculture, computer databanks, and journals in which the information is assumed to be in the public domain. However, many specialty items, new products, and processed foods may not be available from these sources or may vary from the average values used in these profiles. More information on new and/or specific products may be obtained by reading the nutrient labels. Unless otherwise specified, the nutritional profile of these recipes is based on all measurements being level.

- **Artificial sweeteners** vary in use and strength so should be used "to taste," using the recipe ingredients as a guideline. Sweeteners using aspartame (NutraSweet and Equal) should not be used as a sweetener in recipes involving prolonged heating, which reduces the sweet taste. For further information on the use of these sweeteners, refer to the package.
- **Buttermilk**, **sour cream**, and **yogurt** are the types available commercially.
- **Cake mixes** which are prepared using package directions include 3 eggs and 1/2 cup oil.
- **Chicken**, cooked for boning and chopping, has been roasted; this method yields the lowest caloric values.
- **Cottage cheese** is cream-style with 4.2% creaming mixture. Dry curd cottage cheese has no creaming mixture.
- **Eggs** are all large. To avoid raw eggs that may carry salmonella, as in eggnog or 6-week muffin batter, use an equivalent amount of commercial egg substitute.
- **Flour** is unsifted all-purpose flour.
- **Garnishes**, serving suggestions, and other optional information and variations are not included in the profile
- **Margarine** and **butter** are regular, not whipped or presoftened.
- **Milk** is whole milk, 3.5% butterfat. Lowfat milk is 1% butterfat. Evaporated milk is whole milk with 60% of the water removed.
- **Oil** is any type of vegetable cooking oil. Shortening is hydrogenated vegetable shortening.
- **Salt** and other ingredients to taste as noted in the ingredients have not been included in the nutritional profile.
- If a choice of ingredients has been given, the nutritional profile reflects the first option. If a choice of amounts has been given, the nutritional profile reflects the greater amount.

Appetizers, Snacks, and Beverages

Water Hydrant

by Luke Holst
Anthon

Fresh water, Iowa's most precious natural resource, is depicted in this photo by Luke Holst. A nine-year member of the Grant-Go-Getters 4-H Club in Woodbury County, Luke has won several photography awards at the Iowa Educational Media Festival. Luke is the son of Chuck and Sandi Holst.

Appetizers • 11

CHEESE BALLS

1 pound Velveeta cheese, crumbled
4 ounces cream cheese, softened
4 ounces Cheddar cheese, shredded
½ cup margarine, softened
1 (3-ounce) package dried beef
1 onion, grated

- Combine the cheeses, margarine, dried beef and onion in a bowl and mix well.
- Shape into 4 balls. May roll in pecans. Chill, covered, in the refrigerator until serving time.
- Yield: 64 servings.

Approx Per Serving: Cal 55; 79% Calories from Fat; T Fat 5 g; Chol 11 mg; Sod 180 mg; Carbo <1 g; Fiber <1 g; Prot 3 g

Lynn Franzkowiak, Schaller

CHEESE SPREAD

8 ounces cream cheese, softened
1 (5-ounce) jar Kraft Roka Blue Cheese
1 (5-ounce) jar Old English cheese
3 tablespoons mayonnaise
½ to ¾ teaspoon garlic salt

- Blend the cheeses, mayonnaise and garlic salt in a bowl.
- Chill, covered, for several hours before serving.
- Serve on crackers, bread or celery.
- Yield: 30 servings.

Approx Per Serving: Cal 63; 84% Calories from Fat; T Fat 6 g; Chol 15 mg; Sod 187 mg; Carbo 1 g; Fiber 0 g; Prot 2 g

Jenny Christoffersen, Casey

BEEF JERKY

1/4 cup soy sauce
1 tablespoon Worcestershire sauce
1 tablespoon barbecue sauce
1/4 teaspoon pepper
1 tablespoon curry powder
3 pounds rump roast beef

- Combine the soy sauce, Worcestershire sauce, barbecue sauce, pepper and curry powder in a bowl and mix well.
- Cut the beef into 1/8-inch-thick strips. Place in a shallow container. Pour the marinade over the beef. Chill, covered, overnight.
- Place the beef in a single layer in a dehydrator.
- Dehydrate at 145 degrees for 10 to 24 hours or until a test piece cracks but does not break when it is bent. Store the cooled jerky in glass jars or heavy plastic bags.
- Yield: 20 servings.

Approx Per Serving: Cal 82; 31% Calories from Fat; T Fat 3 g; Chol 39 mg; Sod 241 mg; Carbo 1 g; Fiber <1 g; Prot 13 g

Tom Corrington, Cherokee

PICK A PICKLE

12 saltine crackers
1/4 cup mayonnaise
3 cheese slices, cut into quarters
12 pickle slices
2 tablespoons mustard

- Place the crackers on a serving plate.
- Layer the mayonnaise, cheese and pickle slices on each cracker. Top with a dot of mustard.
- Yield: 12 servings.

Approx Per Serving: Cal 66; 73% Calories from Fat; T Fat 5 g; Chol 6 mg; Sod 237 mg; Carbo 3 g; Fiber <1 g; Prot 2 g

Cortney Stanzyk, Waukee

Appetizers • 13

CHEESE PUFF

This is a favorite recipe of my mother's, which she got in California. It won a prize at Milk Made Magic Contest two years ago.

1 cup milk
½ cup butter or margarine
½ teaspoon salt
1 cup flour
4 eggs
8 ounces Cheddar cheese, coarsely shredded
2 teaspoons dry sherry

- Place 1 oven rack in the middle of the oven and the other directly above.
- Bring the milk, butter and salt to a boil in a saucepan over medium heat. Stir in the flour all at once using a wooden spoon. Cook for 1 to 2 minutes or until the mixture leaves the sides of the pan and forms a smooth ball, stirring constantly. Remove from the heat.
- Add the eggs 1 at a time, beating well after each addition. Add the cheese and sherry, stirring until well blended.
- Drop by scant tablespoonfuls 2 inches apart onto 2 lightly greased baking sheets. Place 1 baking sheet on each shelf. Bake at 375 degrees for 18 to 20 minutes or until puffed and golden brown, exchanging the position of the pans after 10 minutes.
- Cool on the baking sheets for 5 minutes. Remove to a wire rack to cool completely.
- May be wrapped airtight and frozen.
- Yield: 24 servings.

Approx Per Serving: Cal 107; 67% Calories from Fat; T Fat 8 g; Chol 56 mg; Sod 234 mg; Carbo 5 g; Fiber <1 g; Prot 4 g

Christina Engel, Waverly

MEXICAN FUDGE

3 eggs
5 ounces enchilada sauce
4 cups shredded Colby-Monterey Jack cheese

- Mix the eggs and enchilada sauce in a bowl.
- Layer 2 cups of the cheese, the egg mixture and the remaining 2 cups cheese in a 9x13-inch glass baking dish.
- Bake at 350 degrees for 20 to 25 minutes.
- Yield: 15 servings.

Approx Per Serving: Cal 115; 73% Calories from Fat; T Fat 9 g; Chol 70 mg; Sod 184 mg; Carbo 1 g; Fiber <1 g; Prot 7 g

Jamie McLain, Pocahontas

HIDDEN VALLEY PINWHEELS

These are great at parties.

16 ounces cream cheese, softened
1 (1-ounce) package ranch salad dressing mix
2 green onions, minced
4 (12-inch) flour tortillas
1 (4-ounce) jar diced pimentos, drained
1 (4-ounce) can diced green chiles, drained
1 (2¼-ounce) can sliced black olives, drained

- Combine the cream cheese, salad dressing mix and green onions in a bowl and mix well. Spread on the tortillas.
- Sprinkle equal amounts of the pimentos, green chiles and olives over the cream cheese mixture. Roll the tortillas tightly to enclose the filling.
- Chill, covered, for 2 hours.
- Cut off each end and discard. Cut the tortillas into 1-inch slices. Arrange cut side down on a serving dish.
- Yield: 40 servings.

Approx Per Serving: Cal 62; 65% Calories from Fat; T Fat 5 g; Chol 13 mg; Sod 152 mg; Carbo 4 g; Fiber <1 g; Prot 1 g

Clayton Geschke, New Hampton

MICROWAVE PORK NACHOS

1 pound mild pork sausage
1 pound Velveeta cheese, cubed
1 (8-ounce) jar salsa
1 (20-ounce) bag tortilla chips

- Crumble the pork sausage into a microwave-safe 1½-quart glass bowl.
- Microwave on High for 5 minutes, stirring after 2½ minutes; drain. Add the cheese and salsa.
- Microwave for 2 to 3 minutes or until the cheese is melted, stirring occasionally.
- Serve with the tortilla chips.
- Yield: 10 servings.

Approx Per Serving: Cal 539; 59% Calories from Fat; T Fat 36 g; Chol 61 mg; Sod 1329 mg; Carbo 38 g; Fiber 4 g; Prot 18 g

Nathan Dohlman, Hampton

Appetizers • 15

NACHO PLATTER

1 (16-ounce) can refried beans
1 (12-ounce) can picante sauce
1 (8-ounce) jar Cheez Whiz
1 (7½-ounce) bag tortilla chips
1½ cups shredded lettuce
1 cup chopped tomato
½ cup sour cream

- Combine the beans and picante sauce in a saucepan. Cook over low heat until thoroughly heated, stirring occasionally.
- Heat the Cheez Whiz in a saucepan over low heat until heated through, stirring frequently.
- Layer the tortilla chips, bean mixture, lettuce, tomato and Cheez Whiz on a serving platter. Top with the sour cream.
- Yield: 8 servings.

Approx Per Serving: Cal 333; 45% Calories from Fat; T Fat 17 g; Chol 23 mg; Sod 1011 mg; Carbo 35 g; Fiber 7 g; Prot 11 g

Jacquie Dammann, Manning

SUPER NACHOS

1½ pounds ground beef
Salt and pepper to taste
1 (16-ounce) can refried beans
1 (4-ounce) can chopped green chiles
1 (8-ounce) jar taco sauce
2 to 3 cups shredded Cheddar cheese
1 onion, chopped
1 cup sour cream
1 (20-ounce) package taco chips

- Brown the ground beef in a skillet, stirring until crumbly; drain. Season to taste.
- Layer the beans, ground beef, green chiles, taco sauce, cheese and onion in the order listed in a 9x13-inch baking dish.
- Bake at 400 degrees for 20 to 25 minutes.
- Serve with sour cream and taco chips.
- Yield: 8 servings.

Approx Per Serving: Cal 846; 53% Calories from Fat; T Fat 51 g; Chol 124 mg; Sod 1516 mg; Carbo 63 g; Fiber 10 g; Prot 40 g

Kristin Hansen, Milford

STUFFED PIZZA BREAD

This is simple and fun for children to make.

1 (1-pound) loaf frozen bread dough, thawed
1 (8-ounce) package sliced pepperoni
1 cup shredded Colby and Monterey Jack cheese

- Roll out the bread dough to a rectangle on a flat surface.
- Place the pepperoni between 2 pieces of paper towel. Microwave for 30 seconds to reduce the fat content.
- Layer the pepperoni and cheese on the bread dough. Roll to enclose, pressing the ends together. Cut into halves.
- Place on a greased baking sheet.
- Bake at 350 degrees for 25 minutes or until golden brown.
- Yield: 4 servings.

Approx Per Serving: Cal 692; 50% Calories from Fat; T Fat 38 g; Chol 71 mg; Sod 1846 mg; Carbo 57 g; Fiber 3 g; Prot 28 g

Alex Broderick, Waukee

VEG-ET POCKETS ❖

1996 Junior Division Purple Ribbon winner of Best of Iowa at the Cass County Fair.

½ cup finely chopped broccoli
½ cup finely chopped cauliflower
4 slices whole wheat bread
2 slices Velveeta cheese

- Preheat a snack-maker. Combine the broccoli and cauliflower in a bowl and mix well.
- Open the snack-maker. Place 1 slice of bread in each side. Add ½ cup of the vegetable mixture and 1 slice cheese to each side. Top each side with the remaining bread.
- Close the snack-maker. Cook for 2 minutes. Open carefully and remove the pockets.
- Yield: 2 servings.

Approx Per Serving: Cal 260; 27% Calories from Fat; T Fat 8 g; Chol 13 mg; Sod 638 mg; Carbo 38 g; Fiber 7 g; Prot 13 g

Bethany Rogers, Wiota

BEAN DIP

1 pound ground beef
1 (16-ounce) can refried beans
1 (4-ounce) can chopped green chiles
1 (15-ounce) can Manwich
1 (16-ounce) jar Cheez Whiz

- Brown the ground beef in a skillet, stirring until crumbly; drain.
- Add the beans, chiles, Manwich and Cheez Whiz. Heat to serving temperature.
- Serve with chips.
- Yield: 20 servings.

Approx Per Serving: Cal 151; 49% Calories from Fat; T Fat 8 g; Chol 29 mg; Sod 598 mg; Carbo 9 g; Fiber 2 g; Prot 10 g

Clayton Geschke, New Hampton

HAMBURGER DIP

I presented this recipe for the Pride of Iowa Contest at our local fair and received a blue ribbon.

1½ pounds ground beef
1 medium onion, chopped
¼ cup barbecue sauce
1¼ teaspoons chili powder
¼ teaspoon salt
1 (8-ounce) can bean dip
¼ cup chopped onion
¼ cup sliced stuffed olives
½ cup shredded Cheddar cheese

- Brown the ground beef with the onion in a skillet, stirring until crumbly; drain. Add the barbecue sauce, chili powder, salt and bean dip, mixing well.
- Spoon into a chafing dish or small electric skillet. Layer the onion, olives and cheese over the ground beef mixture.
- Heat, covered, on low until the cheese melts.
- Serve with butter crackers or corn chips.
- Yield: 15 servings.

Approx Per Serving: Cal 146; 54% Calories from Fat; T Fat 9 g; Chol 38 mg; Sod 354 mg; Carbo 4 g; Fiber 1 g; Prot 12 g

Robert Denger, Dows

HOT HAMBURGER DIP

1 pound ground beef
1 (16-ounce) can refried beans
1 to 1½ cups salsa
16 ounces cream cheese, sliced
1 cup shredded Cheddar cheese

- Brown the ground beef in a skillet, stirring until crumbly; drain. Add the beans and salsa, mixing well. Pour into a 10-inch glass baking dish.
- Layer the slices of cream cheese over the top and sprinkle with the Cheddar cheese.
- Bake at 350 degrees for 15 to 20 minutes or until the cheese is melted.
- Serve with warm tortilla chips.
- Yield: 20 servings.

Approx Per Serving: Cal 182; 65% Calories from Fat; T Fat 13 g; Chol 48 mg; Sod 294 mg; Carbo 6 g; Fiber 2 g; Prot 10 g

Kristin Boswell, Waukee

OYSTER CRACKER SNACK

My family enjoys this snack and it is so easy to make. We always make it for New Year's Eve.

1 cup vegetable oil
1 package ranch salad dressing mix
½ teaspoon lemon juice
½ teaspoon dillweed
½ teaspoon garlic powder
2 (14-ounce) packages oyster crackers

- Combine the oil, salad dressing mix, lemon juice, dillweed and garlic powder in a bowl and mix well.
- Combine the oyster crackers and the oil mixture in a large container, tossing to coat. Store in a covered container.
- May also use this mixture to coat popped popcorn.
- Yield: 16 servings.

Approx Per Serving: Cal 340; 52% Calories from Fat; T Fat 20 g; Chol 0 mg; Sod 766 mg; Carbo 37 g; Fiber 1 g; Prot 5 g

Katie Winston, Atlantic

---

*Macala Rush, Griswold, makes **Granola Bars** by warming ½ cup honey and ½ cup peanut butter and mixing well. Add with 1 teaspoon vanilla extract to 5 cups Favorite Granola (page 21) and mix well. Spread in a large pan. Cut into 12 bars. Store, wrapped, in the freezer.*

Snacks • 19

FLAMME SPECIAL

This easy-to-make snack is a club favorite for overnights. It is also a favorite of family and friends and is a welcome gift.

6 quarts popped popcorn
1/2 cup slivered almonds
1/2 to 1 cup coarsely chopped pecans
1 1/3 cups sugar
1 cup margarine
1/2 cup light corn syrup
1 teaspoon vanilla extract

- Remove any unpopped kernels from the popped popcorn. Combine the popcorn, almonds and pecans in a large container.
- Combine the sugar, margarine and corn syrup in a saucepan. Cook over medium heat until the sugar is dissolved, stirring constantly. Bring to a boil. Cook for 10 to 15 minutes or until light brown and 234 to 240 degrees on a candy thermometer, soft-ball stage. Stir in the vanilla.
- Add to the popcorn mixture, stirring with a long wooden spoon until the popcorn is lightly coated. Cool the mixture.
- Break into serving size pieces and store in an airtight container.
- Do not use fat-free margarine in this recipe.
- Yield: 24 servings.

Approx Per Serving: Cal 211; 52% Calories from Fat; T Fat 13 g; Chol 0 mg; Sod 98 mg; Carbo 24 g; Fiber 2 g; Prot 2 g

Pauline Flamme, Gladbrook

PEANUT BUTTER POPCORN

1 bag microwave popcorn
1/2 cup sugar
1/2 cup light corn syrup
1/2 cup peanut butter
1/2 teaspoon vanilla extract

- Microwave the popcorn using the package directions.
- Bring the sugar and corn syrup to a rolling boil in a saucepan over medium heat, stirring frequently. Remove from the heat.
- Stir in the peanut butter and vanilla. Pour over the hot popped popcorn in a bowl, mixing well.
- Yield: 8 servings.

Approx Per Serving: Cal 250; 35% Calories from Fat; T Fat 10 g; Chol 0 mg; Sod 312 mg; Carbo 38 g; Fiber 2 g; Prot 5 g

R. Crotty, Klemme

POPCORN BALLS

4 cups miniature marshmallows
1/2 cup margarine
1/2 teaspoon vanilla extract
1/4 teaspoon salt
5 quarts popped popcorn

- Combine the marshmallows, margarine, vanilla and salt in a saucepan. Cook over medium heat until the marshmallows are melted, stirring frequently.
- Pour over the popped popcorn in a bowl, mixing well. Cool the mixture slightly.
- Shape with buttered hands into balls.
- May add food coloring if desired.
- Yield: 18 servings.

Approx Per Serving: Cal 112; 43% Calories from Fat; T Fat 5 g; Chol 0 mg; Sod 94 mg; Carbo 15 g; Fiber 1 g; Prot 1 g

Brooke Cornelius, Parkersburg

PARTY POPCORN

This has been a favorite in our family since I was a little girl. Now that I am in college, it is one of those special snacks I request from home.

6 quarts popped popcorn
1 1/2 cups dry-roasted peanuts
1 cup sugar
1/2 cup honey
1/2 cup light corn syrup
1 cup peanut butter
1 teaspoon vanilla extract

- Remove any unpopped kernels from the popped popcorn. Combine the popcorn and peanuts in a large roasting pan. Keep warm in a 250-degree oven.
- Butter the side of a heavy 1 1/2 quart saucepan. Combine the sugar, honey and corn syrup in the saucepan. Bring the mixture to a boil over medium heat, stirring constantly. Boil for 2 minutes, stirring frequently. Remove from the heat.
- Stir in the peanut butter and vanilla. Pour over the popcorn mixture, stirring to coat. Cool the mixture.
- Break into serving pieces.
- Yield: 24 servings.

Approx Per Serving: Cal 220; 39% Calories from Fat; T Fat 10 g; Chol 0 mg; Sod 60 mg; Carbo 30 g; Fiber 3 g; Prot 6 g

Jill Asmus, Webster City

Snacks • 21

FAVORITE GRANOLA

My mom has tried many granola recipes but when she found this one we all loved it.

4 cups rolled oats
2 cups rolled wheat
1 cup unprocessed oat or wheat bran
1 cup whole wheat flour
1/2 cup nonfat dry milk powder
1/2 teaspoon salt
1/2 to 1 cup sunflower seed kernels
1 to 2 cups slivered almonds
1 teaspoon vanilla extract
1/2 cup vegetable oil
1 cup water
3/4 cup packed brown sugar
1 cup raisins
1 cup chopped dried apples or pineapple
1 cup shredded coconut

- Combine the oats, wheat, bran, flour, dry milk powder, salt, sunflower seed kernels and almonds in a large bowl and mix well.
- Process the vanilla, oil, water and brown sugar in a blender until well mixed. Pour over the oats mixture, tossing lightly to mix. Spread on a large baking sheet.
- Bake at 200 degrees for 1 to 1 1/2 hours or until golden brown. For chunky granola do not stir during baking.
- Break into bite-size pieces. Add the raisins, dried apples and coconut, mixing well. Store in an airtight container.
- Yield: 30 servings.

Approx Per Serving: Cal 250; 43% Calories from Fat; T Fat 13 g; Chol <1 mg; Sod 49 mg; Carbo 31 g; Fiber 5 g; Prot 7 g

Macala Rush, Griswold

CARAMEL CORN

1 cup margarine or butter
2 cups sugar
1/2 cup dark corn syrup
1/2 teaspoon salt
1/2 teaspoon baking soda
6 quarts unsalted popped popcorn

- Combine the margarine, sugar, corn syrup and salt in a saucepan. Bring to a boil over medium heat, stirring occasionally. Cook for 5 minutes or to 240 to 248 degrees on a candy thermometer, firm-ball stage, stirring frequently. Remove from the heat.
- Add the baking soda, beating well. Pour over the popped popcorn in a bowl, stirring to coat.
- Spread on a large baking sheet. Bake at 250 degrees for 1 hour, stirring occasionally.
- Yield: 20 servings.

Approx Per Serving: Cal 219; 38% Calories from Fat; T Fat 10 g; Chol 0 mg; Sod 194 mg; Carbo 34 g; Fiber 1 g; Prot 1 g

Stephanie Gorball, Osceola

CARAMEL MIX

This recipe was the Junior Top of Class in the 1995 "Promote Our Commodities" at the Franklin County Fair.

1 cup soybeans
Seasoned salt to taste
²/₃ cup soybean margarine
²/₃ cup packed brown sugar
6 cups Crispix cereal

- Cover the soybeans with at least 2 inches of water in a saucepan. Bring to a boil. Remove from the heat. Let stand overnight. Drain and pat dry with paper towels. Spread in 1 layer in a 9x13-inch microwave-safe baking dish sprayed with nonstick baking spray. Sprinkle lightly with seasoned salt.
- Microwave on High for 7 minutes; stir. Microwave for 5 minutes; stir. Microwave for 3 minutes; stir. Microwave for 30- to 60-second intervals until the soybeans are crisp, stirring frequently.
- Combine the margarine and brown sugar in a saucepan. Boil for 1 minute, stirring frequently.
- Place the cereal and roasted soybeans on a baking sheet. Pour the brown sugar mixture over the mixture, stirring lightly.
- Bake at 350 degrees for 18 minutes, stirring after 9 minutes. Pour into a nonrecycled brown paper bag and cool.
- Yield: 14 servings.

Approx Per Serving: Cal 204; 44% Calories from Fat; T Fat 10 g; Chol 0 mg; Sod 170 mg; Carbo 23 g; Fiber 3 g; Prot 6 g

Nathaniel Johansen, Hampton

PUPPY CHOW

We eat this up fast. It is a fun snack to have.

½ cup margarine
½ cup peanut butter
1 cup chocolate chips
8 cups Rice Chex or Crispix cereal
2 cups confectioners' sugar

- Microwave the margarine, peanut butter and chocolate chips in a microwave-safe bowl until melted, stirring to blend.
- Combine the cereal and chocolate mixture in a large bowl, tossing to coat.
- Combine the cereal and confectioners' sugar in a large covered container or nonrecycled paper bag. Shake to mix well. Spread on waxed paper to dry.
- Yield: 10 servings.

Approx Per Serving: Cal 411; 44% Calories from Fat; T Fat 21 g; Chol 0 mg; Sod 337 mg; Carbo 55 g; Fiber 3 g; Prot 5 g

David and Daniel Oswald, Fredericksburg

Beverages • 23

CASHEW MIX

Over twenty years ago my grandfather, Rex McMahill, clipped this recipe from Mary Bryson's column in the Des Moines Register. *It is the favorite snack of all who visit our home.*

8 cups golden graham cereal
2 (12-ounce) cans cashew halves
½ cup butter or margarine
½ cup grated Parmesan cheese
½ teaspoon seasoned salt
½ teaspoon celery salt
½ teaspoon oregano

- Spread the cereal and cashews in a 10x15-inch baking pan.
- Combine the butter, cheese and seasonings in a saucepan. Cook until the butter and cheese are melted, stirring constantly. Drizzle over the cereal mixture.
- Bake at 225 degrees for 10 minutes. Stir the mixture. Bake for 10 minutes longer. Stir and cool.
- Store in an airtight container.
- Yield: 16 servings.

Approx Per Serving: Cal 385; 62% Calories from Fat; T Fat 28 g; Chol 18 mg; Sod 404 mg; Carbo 29 g; Fiber 4 g; Prot 9 g

Margo McMahill, Ankeny

ANGEL FROST ❖

1 (6-ounce) can frozen pink lemonade concentrate, thawed
1 cup milk
1 (10-ounce) package frozen strawberries in syrup, partially thawed
1 pint vanilla ice cream

- Process the lemonade concentrate, milk, strawberries and ice cream in a blender until puréed.
- Pour into glasses. Garnish with fresh strawberries.
- Yield: 4 servings.

Approx Per Serving: Cal 302; 27% Calories from Fat; T Fat 9 g; Chol 37 mg; Sod 85 mg; Carbo 53 g; Fiber 2 g; Prot 5 g

Nick Franzkowiak, Schaller

BANANA YOGURT DRINK ❖

I took this recipe to the Shelby County Milk Made Magic Contest in 1993 and won in the Young Chefs Snacks category. I was chosen to give a presentation on the recipe at the Iowa State Fair where I got first place in the Young Chefs Snacks category and received $125.

2 ripe medium bananas
2 cups milk
1 cup strawberry yogurt
8 ice cubes

- Cut the bananas into chunks.
- Process the milk, yogurt and ice cubes in a blender briefly. Add the banana. Process for 30 seconds or until smooth. Garnish with fresh strawberries.
- Yield: 4 servings.

Approx Per Serving: Cal 190; 26% Calories from Fat; T Fat 6 g; Chol 17 mg; Sod 95 mg; Carbo 30 g; Fiber 1 g; Prot 7 g

Emily Bruck, Earling

BERRY BANANA SMOOTHIE ❖

1 small banana, cut up and frozen
1/4 cup fresh or frozen assorted berries
1 cup orange juice
3 tablespoons low-fat vanilla yogurt

- Process the banana, berries, orange juice and yogurt in a blender until smooth.
- Pour into tall glasses. Garnish with fresh sliced strawberries.
- Yield: 2 servings.

Approx Per Serving: Cal 122; 6% Calories from Fat; T Fat 1 g; Chol 1 mg; Sod 17 mg; Carbo 28 g; Fiber 2 g; Prot 3 g

Amanda Wood, Pocahontas

FRUIT SMOOTHIE ❖

1 banana
1 cup apple juice
1 cup orange juice
1/4 cup crushed pineapple
1 teaspoon sugar
Ice as needed

- Process the banana, fruit juices, pineapple, sugar and ice in a blender until smooth.
- Pour into glasses and enjoy!
- Yield: 4 servings.

Approx Per Serving: Cal 96; 3% Calories from Fat; T Fat <1 g; Chol 0 mg; Sod 3 mg; Carbo 24 g; Fiber 1 g; Prot 1 g

Julie Gonnerman, Waukee

Beverages • 25

HOT BUTTERED ICE CREAM MIX

1 quart vanilla ice
  cream, softened
1 (1-pound) package
  brown sugar
1½ cups butter,
  softened

- Combine the ice cream, brown sugar and butter in a mixer bowl. Beat until well blended.
- Store in an airtight container in the freezer.
- Place 2 teaspoons mix in a cup. Fill with boiling water.
- Will keep several weeks in the freezer.
- Yield: 186 servings.

Approx Per Serving: Cal 28; 56% Calories from Fat; T Fat 2 g; Chol 5 mg; Sod 18 mg; Carbo 3 g; Fiber <1 g; Prot <1 g

Michaela Lauritsen, Exira

ORANGE FROSTY

I wanted something cold on a hot day so I made a new recipe.

1 quart frozen orange
  juice concentrate
2 to 2½ cups water
3 cups ice

- Process the orange juice concentrate, water and ice in a blender until the ice is crushed.
- Pour into glasses.
- Yield: 5 servings.

Approx Per Serving: Cal 362; 1% Calories from Fat; T Fat <1 g; Chol 0 mg; Sod 7 mg; Carbo 87 g; Fiber 2 g; Prot 5 g

Erin Pierce, Ogden

SLUSHY FRUITIES ❖

This is a wonderful cool fat-free snack in the summer.

12 ounces frozen orange
  juice concentrate
12 ounces frozen
  lemonade concentrate
1 (20-ounce) can
  crushed pineapple
2 (12-ounce) cans
  lemon-lime soda
1 (10-ounce) package
  frozen strawberries
1 or 2 bananas, sliced

- Process the orange juice and lemonade concentrates, pineapple, lemon-lime soda, strawberries and bananas in a blender until well mixed. Pour into individual plastic cups. Seal with a top. Store in the freezer.
- Loosen the top. Microwave for 1 minute to thaw. Stir until slushy.
- Yield: 12 servings.

Approx Per Serving: Cal 181; 1% Calories from Fat; T Fat <1 g; Chol 0 mg; Sod 9 mg; Carbo 46 g; Fiber 2 g; Prot 1 g

Wendy White, Hornick

GOURMET FLAVORED COCOA MIX ❖

When you buy store-brand ingredients, this figures about nine cents per serving, which is much less expensive than the small packets of flavored cocoa mix. A jar of this makes a wonderful Christmas present.

- 1 (8-quart) package nonfat dry milk powder
- 1 (2-pound) package chocolate instant drink mix
- 1 (16-ounce) jar nondairy creamer
- 1 (1-pound) package confectioners' sugar
- 1 (8-ounce) jar flavored creamer

- Combine the dry milk powder, drink mix, creamer, confectioners' sugar and flavored creamer in a large container and mix well. Store in an airtight container.
- Place 3 tablespoons mix in a mug. Stir in 8 ounces boiling water.
- Yield: 100 servings.

Approx Per Serving: Cal 159; 13% Calories from Fat; T Fat 2 g; Chol 4 mg; Sod 147 mg; Carbo 28 g; Fiber 1 g; Prot 8 g

Janet Summy, Crescent

MOCHA INSTANT MIX ❖

I gave this to Mom for Christmas when I was in Mrs. DeWall's second grade class. My sister, Emily, used this recipe for a 4-H project to compare the cost of homemade mocha mix and store-bought. This is much more economical.

- 1½ cups nondairy creamer
- 1½ cups nonfat dry milk powder
- 1½ cups packed brown sugar
- ½ cup confectioners' sugar
- ¾ cup baking cocoa
- ¼ cup plus 2 tablespoons instant coffee powder
- 1⅔ cups miniature marshmallows

- Combine the creamer, dry milk powder, brown sugar, confectioners' sugar, baking cocoa and instant coffee in a large container and mix well. Sift once. Stir in the marshmallows. Store in an airtight container.
- Place 3 tablespoons mix in a mug and add boiling water.
- Yield: 40 servings.

Approx Per Serving: Cal 64; 15% Calories from Fat; T Fat 1 g; Chol <1 mg; Sod 25 mg; Carbo 13 g; Fiber <1 g; Prot 1 g

Sarah Baade, Havelock

Soups and Salads

Barn Scene

by Mandy Herren
Monticello

Mandy Herren focuses on the age and beauty of the Iowa countryside with her picture. Mandy belongs to the Scotch Grove Challengers 4-H Club in Jones County. She has been exploring the photography project for five years. Mandy's parents are Chris and Kelly Herren.

DR PEPPER BEEF STEW

3 pounds stew beef
  cubes
1 tablespoon salt
1 teaspoon black pepper
1/4 cup flour
3 tablespoons vegetable
  oil
2 cups beef stock or
  bouillon
2 cups Dr Pepper
2 cups coarsely chopped
  carrots
3 cups coarsely chopped
  potatoes
1 1/2 cups coarsely
  chopped onions
1 cup chopped celery
1 cup frozen green peas

- Season the beef with salt and pepper; dust with flour.
- Brown the beef in the oil in a large stockpot. Add the beef stock and Dr Pepper. Cook over low heat until tender, stirring occasionally.
- Add the carrots, potatoes, onions and celery.
- Cook until the vegetables are tender, stirring occasionally. Add the green peas. Cook for 10 minutes longer.
- Yield: 6 servings.

Approx Per Serving: Cal 541; 38% Calories from Fat; T Fat 23 g; Chol 136 mg; Sod 5119 mg; Carbo 36 g; Fiber 4 g; Prot 47 g

LeAnn Kaster, Hull

ELEPHANT STEW

A 4-H favorite from Minnesota, adapted from Larry Goelz. I "herd" there were elephants in Iowa, too!

1 medium elephant
Brown gravy
16 ounces medium egg
  noodles
Salt and pepper to taste
2 rabbits

- Dice the elephant into small cubes. Place in a 4-ton baking dish. Allow 60 days for this process. Add enough brown gravy to cover.
- Bake at 325 degrees for 4 weeks.
- Cook the noodles using the package directions; drain. Mix with the elephant stew.
- Season to taste and serve hot.
- If your guests are really hungry, add 2 rabbits but only if necessary as most people do not like "hare" in their stew.
- Yield: 3,652 servings.

Nutritional information for this recipe is not available.

Albert Grunenwald, Development Assistant, Iowa 4-H Foundation

FOOTBALL STEW ❖

A wonderful recipe for the oven while you attend an ISU or UNI football game or a 4-H activity.

2 cups tomato juice
3 tablespoons tapioca
1 tablespoon sugar
1½ teaspoons salt
1 tablespoon Worcestershire sauce
2 pounds stew beef cubes
2 cups chopped peeled potatoes
2 cups chopped celery
2 cups chopped carrots
1 onion, chopped

- Combine the first 5 ingredients in a bowl and mix well.
- Combine the beef and vegetables in a roasting pan. Add the tomato juice mixture, stirring well.
- Bake, covered, at 250 degrees for 5 hours.
- May also cook in a slow cooker on High for 1 hour. Reduce the temperature to Low and cook for 5 to 6 hours or to 160 degrees on a meat thermometer.
- Yield: 10 servings.

Approx Per Serving: Cal 187; 30% Calories from Fat; T Fat 6 g; Chol 54 mg; Sod 700 mg; Carbo 15 g; Fiber 2 g; Prot 18 g

Don Goering, Extension Youth Development Specialist

CHEESY CHOWDER

1 cup chopped potatoes
½ cup chopped carrots
½ cup chopped celery
½ cup chopped onion
½ cup chopped green bell pepper
¼ cup butter
3 cups chicken broth
⅛ teaspoon pepper
½ cup flour
2 cups milk
3 cups shredded Velveeta, American or sharp Cheddar cheese

- Cook the potatoes, carrots, celery, onion and green pepper in the butter in a large stockpot until tender, stirring frequently.
- Add the chicken broth and pepper. Simmer, covered, for 30 minutes, stirring occasionally.
- Blend the flour and milk together in a bowl until smooth. Add to the chowder and mix well. Stir in the cheese. Cook until thickened and bubbly, stirring frequently.
- Yield: 6 servings.

Approx Per Serving: Cal 418; 62% Calories from Fat; T Fat 29 g; Chol 85 mg; Sod 1329 mg; Carbo 20 g; Fiber 1 g; Prot 20 g

Kelley Hartwick, Bloomfield

Soups • 31

CHEESE SOUP

This soup is better the third day. It is our favorite supper for Christmas Eve.

4 cups chopped potatoes
1 cup chopped carrots
1 cup chopped celery
¾ teaspoon salt
4 cups water
½ cup margarine
½ cup flour
4 cups milk
1 pound Velveeta cheese, crumbled
2 cups chopped cooked ham

- Combine the potatoes, carrots, celery, salt and water in a saucepan. Cook over medium heat until the vegetables are tender, stirring occasionally.
- Microwave the margarine in a microwave-safe bowl until melted. Stir in the flour until smooth.
- Microwave for 3 minutes and whip well. Add 1 cup milk.
- Microwave for 1 minute and whip well. Add the remaining milk 1 cup at a time, microwaving for 1 minute after each addition and whipping well.
- Add the white sauce, cheese and ham to the vegetables, mixing well. Heat to serving temperature but do not boil.
- Yield: 6 servings.

Approx Per Serving: Cal 715; 59% Calories from Fat; T Fat 47 g; Chol 119 mg; Sod 2251 mg; Carbo 37 g; Fiber 3 g; Prot 37 g

Rachael Thompson, Sac City

VEGETABLE CHEESE SOUP

3 cups finely chopped potatoes
½ cup finely chopped broccoli
¼ cup chopped onion
½ cup chopped celery
½ cup thinly sliced carrots
½ cup finely chopped ham
1 cup water
½ teaspoon salt
1 teaspoon parsley flakes
1 chicken bouillon cube
⅛ teaspoon white pepper
1½ cups milk
2 tablespoons flour
8 ounces Velveeta cheese, cubed

- Combine the vegetables, ham, water, salt, parsley flakes, bouillon cube and white pepper in a stockpot. Cook over medium heat until the vegetables are tender, stirring occasionally and adding additional water as needed.
- Combine the milk and flour in a bowl and mix well. Stir into the soup.
- Place the cheese in a microwave-safe bowl. Microwave until melted. Add to the soup. Heat to serving temperature.
- Yield: 6 servings.

Approx Per Serving: Cal 276; 47% Calories from Fat; T Fat 15 g; Chol 51 mg; Sod 1112 mg; Carbo 21 g; Fiber 2 g; Prot 16 g

Brianna Delphey, Waukee

CANADIAN CHEESE SOUP WITH POPCORN

The Lester Livewires Senior Club has used this recipe for the last two years for our Senior Citizens' Meal.

1 (10-ounce) package frozen mixed vegetables
1 (20-ounce) package frozen cauliflower
Salt to taste
2 (10-ounce) cans celery soup
2 (10-ounce) cans chicken soup
1 (12-ounce) can evaporated milk
3 cups milk
1 pound Velveeta cheese, crumbled
1/3 cup Cheez Whiz
1 bag microwave popcorn, popped

- Cook the mixed vegetables and cauliflower with salt to taste using the package directions; drain.
- Combine the celery soup, chicken soup, evaporated milk, milk, Velveeta cheese and Cheez Whiz in a large saucepan, mixing well.
- Add the vegetables to the soup. Simmer for 15 minutes, stirring occasionally.
- Serve topped with the popped popcorn.
- Yield: 8 servings.

Approx Per Serving: Cal 565; 57% Calories from Fat; T Fat 37 g; Chol 99 mg; Sod 2452 mg; Carbo 35 g; Fiber 3 g; Prot 27 g

Katie Mostek, Dunkerton

CREAM OF BROCCOLI SOUP

Florets of 1 pound fresh or frozen broccoli
1/2 cup water
1 cup butter or margarine
1 cup sifted flour
1 quart chicken stock
1 quart half-and-half
1 teaspoon salt
1/4 teaspoon pepper

- Cut the broccoli into 1/2-inch pieces. Place in a saucepan with the water. Simmer until tender-crisp. Do not drain.
- Melt the butter in a 4- to 6-quart saucepan over medium heat. Stir in the flour. Simmer for 2 to 4 minutes, whisking constantly. Add the chicken stock. Bring to boil, whisking constantly. Reduce the heat to low. Add the broccoli, half-and-half, salt and pepper. Heat to serving temperature. Do not boil.
- May substitute 4 chicken bouillon cubes dissolved in 1 quart hot water for the chicken stock.
- Yield: 10 servings.

Approx Per Serving: Cal 351; 76% Calories from Fat; T Fat 30 g; Chol 85 mg; Sod 756 mg; Carbo 14 g; Fiber 1 g; Prot 7 g

Karen Knight, State Youth and 4-H Staff

Soups • 33

FAVORITE SOUP ❖

2 quarts water
2 tablespoons chicken broth
2 tablespoons parsley flakes
2 to 3 potatoes, chopped
2 to 3 carrots, chopped
1 (16-ounce) package frozen broccoli
1/2 cup broken uncooked spaghetti
1 (26-ounce) can chicken with rice soup

- Combine the water, chicken broth, parsley flakes, potatoes and carrots in a 6-quart saucepan. Cook over medium heat until the vegetables are tender, stirring occasionally.
- Add the broccoli and spaghetti. Cook until tender, stirring occasionally.
- Add the canned soup. Heat to serving temperature.
- Yield: 10 servings.

Approx Per Serving: Cal 112; 11% Calories from Fat; T Fat 1 g; Chol 4 mg; Sod 521 mg; Carbo 21 g; Fiber 3 g; Prot 5 g

Alissa Kattenberg, Hull

FOUR-ONION SOUP

1 medium yellow onion
1 medium red onion
5 green onions with tops
White portion of 1 medium leek
1 clove of garlic, minced
2 tablespoons butter or margarine
2 (14-ounce) cans beef broth
1 (10-ounce) can beef consommé
1 teaspoon Worcestershire sauce
1/2 teaspoon ground nutmeg
4 ounces Swiss cheese, shredded
6 (3/4-inch-thick) slices French bread
6 tablespoons grated Parmesan cheese

- Cut the onions and the leek into 1/4-inch-thick slices. Sauté the onions and garlic in the butter in a 3-quart saucepan for 15 minutes or until golden brown. Add the broth, consommé, Worcestershire sauce and nutmeg. Bring to a boil over medium heat. Reduce the heat to low.
- Simmer, covered, for 30 minutes, stirring occasionally.
- Sprinkle 1 tablespoon Swiss cheese in each of six 8-ounce bowls. Ladle the hot soup into the bowls. Top each with French bread and sprinkle with the remaining Swiss cheese and Parmesan cheese.
- Broil under a hot broiler until the cheese melts. Serve immediately.
- Yield: 6 servings.

Approx Per Serving: Cal 290; 39% Calories from Fat; T Fat 13 g; Chol 33 mg; Sod 1660 mg; Carbo 28 g; Fiber 2 g; Prot 18 g

Jennifer Knupp, Washington

POTATO SOUP

8 to 10 medium potatoes, peeled, cubed
2 medium onions, coarsely chopped
2 teaspoons salt
1 (5-ounce) can evaporated milk
1 (10-ounce) can cream of celery soup
½ cup margarine

- Place the potatoes and onions in a saucepan with enough water to reach 2 inches below the top of the saucepan. Add the salt. Cook until the vegetables are tender, stirring occasionally. Drain, reserving the liquid.
- Add the evaporated milk and celery soup to the cooked vegetables, mixing well. Fill the milk can and soup can with the reserved liquid. Add to the saucepan with the margarine. Heat to serving temperature.
- Yield: 8 servings.

Approx Per Serving: Cal 305; 42% Calories from Fat; T Fat 15 g; Chol 9 mg; Sod 983 mg; Carbo 40 g; Fiber 3 g; Prot 5 g

Wendy Handy, Fremont County

TACO SOUP

1 pound ground beef
1 package taco seasoning mix
1 (8-ounce) can whole kernel corn, drained
½ cup chopped onion, or to taste
4 cups tomato juice
2 (8-ounce) cans Mexican-style chopped tomatoes

- Brown the ground beef in a skillet, stirring until crumbly; drain. Stir in the taco seasoning mix.
- Combine the ground beef mixture and remaining ingredients in a stockpot. Simmer for 30 minutes, stirring occasionally.
- Serve with taco cheese and crushed cheese nacho chips.
- May substitute dried onion flakes for the onion.
- Yield: 8 servings.

Approx Per Serving: Cal 207; 35% Calories from Fat; T Fat 8 g; Chol 42 mg; Sod 1178 mg; Carbo 19 g; Fiber 2 g; Prot 15 g

Katie Bogue, Ogden

SPECIAL HOT CHILI

My dad made up this recipe about ten years ago. It is very spicy but you can cut the amount of chili powder in half.

1 pound ground beef
¼ cup minced onion
1 (48-ounce) can tomato juice
1 (15-ounce) can tomato sauce
¾ cup minced onion
1 tablespoon Italian seasoning
1 tablespoon pepper
¼ cup chili powder
1 (15-ounce) can pork and beans
6 slices crisp-cooked bacon, crumbled

- Brown the ground beef with ¼ cup onion in a skillet, stirring until the ground beef is crumbly; drain.
- Combine the ground beef mixture and the remaining ingredients in a large stockpot. Bring to a boil over medium heat. Reduce the heat. Simmer, covered, for 30 minutes, stirring occasionally.
- May substitute 24 slices pepperoni for the bacon.
- Yield: 10 servings.

Approx Per Serving: Cal 223; 37% Calories from Fat; T Fat 10 g; Chol 40 mg; Sod 1007 mg; Carbo 22 g; Fiber 6 g; Prot 16 g

Debbie Beall, Urbandale

APPLE SALAD

I like this recipe because it tastes good and is easy to make.

6 apples, chopped
½ cup finely sliced celery
¼ cup chopped pecans
¼ cup raisins
¼ cup confectioners' sugar
½ cup mayonnaise-type salad dressing or mayonnaise

- Combine the apples, celery, pecans and raisins in a bowl.
- Combine the confectioners' sugar and mayonnaise-type salad dressing in a bowl and mix well. Add to the apple mixture and toss to coat. Chill, covered, until serving time.
- Yield: 8 servings.

Approx Per Serving: Cal 174; 38% Calories from Fat; T Fat 8 g; Chol 4 mg; Sod 112 mg; Carbo 28 g; Fiber 3 g; Prot 1 g

Marra Burr, Iowa City

CARAMEL APPLE SALAD

2 (4-ounce) packages vanilla instant pudding mix
2 cups milk
12 ounces whipped topping
5 Granny Smith apples, chopped
6 (1-ounce) Snickers candy bars, cubed

- Combine the pudding mix and milk in a large bowl. Beat until well mixed. Fold in the remaining ingredients. Pour into a serving dish.
- Chill for 1 hour or longer before serving.
- Yield: 8 servings.

Approx Per Serving: Cal 411; 38% Calories from Fat; T Fat 18 g; Chol 11 mg; Sod 454 mg; Carbo 62 g; Fiber 2 g; Prot 5 g

Morgan Welper, Lansing

FRUIT SALAD ❖

This is a nice healthy salad or snack for a large gathering of friends.

2 bananas, sliced
1 unpeeled red apple, chopped
1 unpeeled green apple, chopped
Sections of 2 oranges
1 (8-ounce) can pineapple chunks, drained
1 pint fresh strawberries, sliced
1 cup orange juice
1/2 cup sugar
2 tablespoons cornstarch
1 teaspoon grated lemon peel
Juice of 1 lemon
2 teaspoons grated orange peel

- Layer the fruit in a glass bowl.
- Combine the orange juice, sugar and cornstarch in a saucepan. Cook over medium heat until thickened, stirring constantly. Stir in the lemon peel, lemon juice and orange peel.
- Pour the hot sauce over the layered fruit. Chill, covered, for 1 hour or longer before serving.
- Yield: 20 servings.

Approx Per Serving: Cal 65; 3% Calories from Fat; T Fat <1 g; Chol 0 mg; Sod 1 mg; Carbo 17 g; Fiber 1 g; Prot 1 g

Chase Broderick, Waukee

Salads • 37

GOLD COAST SALAD

2/3 cup vegetable oil
1/3 cup wine vinegar
3 tablespoons honey
1 teaspoon poppy seeds
1/2 teaspoon salt
6 cups salad greens
2 cups orange sections
1 1/2 cups grated carrots
1/2 cup raisins, plumped

- Combine the oil, vinegar, honey, poppy seeds and salt in a jar. Cover and shake well. Chill for several hours to blend the flavors. Chill the salad greens and orange sections.
- Combine the greens, orange sections, carrots and raisins in a bowl. Shake the dressing and pour over the salad. Toss well and serve immediately.
- Yield: 6 servings.

Approx Per Serving: Cal 342; 62% Calories from Fat; T Fat 25 g; Chol 0 mg; Sod 204 mg; Carbo 32 g; Fiber 4 g; Prot 2 g

Jayne Hager Dee, 1995-1996 President, Iowa 4-H Foundation

MOUNTAIN DEW SALAD ❖

My grandma made this salad for my dad when he was growing up and my mother makes it for me, only we substitute fruit cocktail for the pineapple in the original recipe.

2 (3-ounce) packages lemon gelatin
2 cups boiling water
1 (15-ounce) can fruit cocktail, drained
2 bananas, sliced
1 (12-ounce) can Mountain Dew
1 cup whipped topping

- Dissolve the gelatin in the boiling water in a bowl. Stir in the fruit cocktail, bananas and Mountain Dew. Spoon into a 9x9-inch serving dish. Chill until set.
- Spread whipped topping over the top of the salad and cut into servings.
- Yield: 9 servings.

Approx Per Serving: Cal 163; 12% Calories from Fat; T Fat 2 g; Chol 0 mg; Sod 57 mg; Carbo 36 g; Fiber 1 g; Prot 2 g

Tad Lincoln, Stockton

PEACH SALAD

2 (3-ounce) packages peach gelatin
1 (4-ounce) package vanilla pudding and pie filling mix
3 cups water
14 large marshmallows
1 (29-ounce) can sliced peaches

- Combine the gelatin, pudding mix and water in a saucepan. Bring to a boil over medium heat. Add the marshmallows and stir until melted.
- Pour into an 8x8-inch serving dish. Stir in the undrained sliced peaches. Chill until set.
- Yield: 8 servings.

Approx Per Serving: Cal 242; 1% Calories from Fat; T Fat <1 g; Chol 0 mg; Sod 244 mg; Carbo 61 g; Fiber 1 g; Prot 2 g

Rebecca Taylor, Oskaloosa

PINK SALAD

1 (20-ounce) can
 crushed pineapple
1 (3-ounce) package red
 gelatin
16 ounces small curd
 cottage cheese
16 ounces whipped
 topping, or 2 packages
 topping mix

- Combine the undrained pineapple and gelatin in a saucepan. Bring to a boil over medium heat, stirring frequently. Remove from the heat. Cool to room temperature.
- Stir in the cottage cheese and whipped topping. Spoon into a serving bowl. Chill until serving time.
- Yield: 8 servings.

Approx Per Serving: Cal 334; 45% Calories from Fat; T Fat 17 g; Chol 8 mg; Sod 272 mg; Carbo 39 g; Fiber <1 g; Prot 9 g

Debbie Beall, Urbandale

PRETZEL SALAD

Yummy for a bunch of people.

2 cups crushed pretzels
3/4 cup melted
 margarine
1/2 cup sugar
8 ounces cream cheese,
 softened
8 ounces whipped
 topping
1 cup sugar
2 cups pineapple juice
1 (3-ounce) package
 strawberry gelatin
1 (10-ounce) package
 frozen strawberries,
 thawed
1/4 cup crushed pretzels

- Combine 2 cups pretzels, margarine and 1/2 cup sugar in a bowl and mix well. Spread over bottom and up sides of a greased 9x13-inch baking dish.
- Bake at 350 degrees for 10 minutes. Cool to room temperature.
- Combine the cream cheese, whipped topping and 1 cup sugar in a bowl and mix well. Spread over the baked crust.
- Bring the pineapple juice to a boil in a saucepan. Stir in the gelatin until dissolved. Add the strawberries and mix well. Spread over the cream cheese mixture. Sprinkle with the remaining 1/4 cup pretzels. Chill, covered, for 2 hours.
- Yield: 12 servings.

Approx Per Serving: Cal 444; 46% Calories from Fat; T Fat 23 g; Chol 21 mg; Sod 487 mg; Carbo 57 g; Fiber 1 g; Prot 4 g

Henry Kelley, Waukee

Salads • 39

SEVEN-LAYER GELATIN SALAD ❖

1 (3-ounce) package each black cherry, lime, orange, strawberry, cherry, lemon and orange-pineapple gelatin
4½ cups boiling water
4½ cups cold water
1 (12-ounce) can evaporated skim milk
8 ounces low-fat whipped topping

- Dissolve each flavor gelatin in a separate bowl. Dissolve black cherry, lime, orange and strawberry gelatins in ¾ cup boiling water each. Add ¾ cup cold water to each and mix well.
- Dissolve cherry, lemon and orange-pineapple gelatins in ½ cup boiling water each. Add ½ cup cold water and ½ cup evaporated skim milk to each and mix well.
- Pour black cherry gelatin into a glass bowl. Chill for 20 to 30 minutes or until set before adding the next layer. Add the cherry, lime, lemon, orange, orange-pineapple and strawberry gelatin 1 at a time in the order listed, chilling each layer for 20 to 30 minutes or until set before adding the next layer.
- Add the whipped topping just before serving.
- May also prepare in a gelatin mold and unmold onto a serving plate when congealed.
- Yield: 16 servings.

Approx Per Serving: Cal 186; 7% Calories from Fat; T Fat 2 g; Chol 1 mg; Sod 119 mg; Carbo 40 g; Fiber 0 g; Prot 5 g

Lynnette Hauser, State Youth and 4-H Staff

STRAWBERRY SALAD

Came from Great-Grandma of Stratford. It's pretty easy to make and very delicious!

1 (3-ounce) package strawberry gelatin
1 cup boiling water
1 (10-ounce) package frozen strawberries
1 cup applesauce
16 ounces whipped topping
8 ounces cream cheese, softened

- Dissolve the gelatin in the boiling water in a bowl. Stir in the strawberries and applesauce. Pour into a serving dish. Chill for 2 hours or until set.
- Combine the whipped topping and cream cheese in a bowl and mix well. Spread over the gelatin.
- Yield: 12 servings.

Approx Per Serving: Cal 237; 60% Calories from Fat; T Fat 16 g; Chol 21 mg; Sod 84 mg; Carbo 22 g; Fiber 1 g; Prot 3 g

Nicole Wilheim, Woodburn

FRUIT KABOBS ❖

Sections of 1 orange
1 pear, sliced
1 cup sliced strawberries
1 cup sliced peaches
1 cup sliced apples
1 cup sliced plums
1 cup watermelon balls
1/2 cup blueberries
1 cup sliced kiwifruit
1 banana, sliced
1 cup seedless grapes
Juice of 1 lemon

- Combine the fruit in a bowl and add the lemon juice. Toss gently to coat.
- Thread the fruit alternately on skewers and place on a serving dish.
- May serve with yogurt for dipping.
- Yield: 20 servings.

Approx Per Serving: Cal 44; 6% Calories from Fat; T Fat <1 g; Chol 0 mg; Sod 1 mg; Carbo 11 g; Fiber 2 g; Prot 1 g

Tiera R. Wright, Iowa City

BROCCOLI DELIGHT SALAD

4 to 5 cups chopped broccoli, or 1 large bunch
1 cup raisins
1/4 cup finely chopped red onion
10 slices crisp-cooked bacon, crumbled
1 cup sunflower kernels
1/2 cup sugar
1 cup mayonnaise
1 1/2 tablespoons vinegar

- Combine the broccoli, raisins, onion, bacon and sunflower kernels in a large glass bowl and mix well.
- Combine the remaining ingredients in a bowl and mix well. Pour over the broccoli salad and toss lightly to mix.
- Yield: 6 servings.

Approx Per Serving: Cal 633; 65% Calories from Fat; T Fat 48 g; Chol 31 mg; Sod 402 mg; Carbo 47 g; Fiber 5 g; Prot 12 g

LeAnn Kaster, Hull

---

*The 4-H Food and Nutrition Project made 1 3/4 cups of **Creamy Low-Calorie Salad Dressing** by blending 1 cup low-fat cottage cheese with 2 tablespoons lemon juice or vinegar and 1/2 cup tomato juice in a blender or electric mixer. Store, covered, in the refrigerator. They also made 1 cup of **Low-Calorie French Salad Dressing** by mixing in a bowl or a covered jar 1 cup tomato juice, 2 tablespoons lemon juice, 1/4 teaspoon oregano, a pinch of garlic powder and pepper. Store, covered, in the refrigerator.*

Salads • 41

CABBAGE SALAD

1 (3-ounce) package
  ramen noodles
1/4 cup margarine
1/4 cup sunflower kernels
1/2 cup slivered almonds
1/4 cup vinegar
1/2 cup sugar
3 tablespoons soy sauce
Salt and pepper to taste
1 small head cabbage
3 bunches green onions

- Reserve the ramen noodles seasoning packet. Crumble the noodles in a skillet. Add the margarine, sunflower kernels and almonds. Sauté until light brown.
- Combine the reserved seasoning packet, vinegar, sugar, soy sauce, salt and pepper in a bowl and mix well.
- Chop the cabbage and green onions. Combine with the noodle mixture and vinegar mixture in a large bowl and toss to mix. Chill before serving.
- Yield: 8 servings.

Approx Per Serving: Cal 263; 48% Calories from Fat; T Fat 15 g; Chol 0 mg; Sod 707 mg; Carbo 30 g; Fiber 4 g; Prot 6 g

Nancy Elmer, Mt. Ayr

CAULIFLOWER LETTUCE SALAD

12 ounces bacon
1 head lettuce
Florets of 1 head
  cauliflower
1 bunch green onions,
  chopped
1/2 cup grated Parmesan
  cheese
1 1/2 cups mayonnaise
1/4 cup sugar

- Cook the bacon until very crisp; drain and crumble.
- Tear the lettuce into bite-size pieces.
- Combine the cauliflower, lettuce and green onions in a large bowl.
- Mix the cheese, mayonnaise and sugar in a bowl. Spread over the salad. Chill, covered, until serving time. Toss to mix just before serving.
- Yield: 8 servings.

Approx Per Serving: Cal 448; 82% Calories from Fat; T Fat 41 g; Chol 40 mg; Sod 578 mg; Carbo 13 g; Fiber 2 g; Prot 9 g

Mary Morris, Ames

PASTA SALAD

1 (12-ounce) package
  colored pasta
1 (8-ounce) bottle
  Italian salad dressing
2 small tomatoes,
  coarsely chopped
1/2 cup grated Parmesan
  cheese

- Cook the pasta using the package directions. Drain and cool.
- Combine the pasta and dressing and toss to mix. Add the tomatoes and mix. Sprinkle the cheese over the pasta and stir to mix. Chill until serving time.
- Yield: 8 servings.

Approx Per Serving: Cal 316; 46% Calories from Fat; T Fat 16 g; Chol 5 mg; Sod 353 mg; Carbo 35 g; Fiber 1 g; Prot 9 g

Emily Davey, Crawfordsville

CREAMY POTATO SALAD

10 pounds potatoes, peeled
6 eggs
2 1/4 cups sugar
6 tablespoons flour
2 teaspoons dry mustard
1 tablespoon salt
1/2 cup vinegar
1 1/2 cups whipping cream
1 cup sour cream
1 cup mayonnaise

- Chop the potatoes into bite-size pieces. Combine the potatoes and water to cover in a large saucepan. Cook over medium heat until the potatoes are tender, stirring occasionally. Cool to room temperature.
- Combine the eggs, sugar, flour, dry mustard, salt, vinegar and whipping cream in a saucepan. Cook over low heat until thickened, stirring constantly. Cool to room temperature. Stir in the sour cream and mayonnaise.
- Combine the potatoes and dressing in a large bowl and toss to mix. Chill until serving time.
- May also add chopped celery, chopped onion, grated carrots and chopped hard-cooked eggs.
- Yield: 32 servings.

Approx Per Serving: Cal 310; 35% Calories from Fat; T Fat 12 g; Chol 62 mg; Sod 266 mg; Carbo 47 g; Fiber 2 g; Prot 5 g

Kyle Cleveringa, Alton

GERMAN POTATO SALAD ❖

1 cup diced bacon
1 cup diced celery
1 cup chopped onion
1 tablespoon salt
3 tablespoons flour
2/3 cup sugar
2/3 cup vinegar
1/2 teaspoon pepper
1 1/3 cups water
8 cups sliced potatoes, cooked

- Sauté the bacon in a large skillet until crisp. Remove the bacon and set aside. Drain the skillet, reserving 1/4 cup bacon drippings.
- Add the celery, onion, salt and flour to the bacon drippings. Simmer gently until well mixed, stirring constantly. Add the sugar, vinegar, pepper and water. Bring to a boil.
- Combine the bacon, potatoes and dressing in a bowl and mix well. Pour into a 3-quart baking dish.
- Bake, covered, at 350 degrees for 30 minutes.
- May also cook in a slow cooker until of serving temperature.
- Yield: 12 servings.

Approx Per Serving: Cal 185; 24% Calories from Fat; T Fat 5 g; Chol 7 mg; Sod 632 mg; Carbo 33 g; Fiber 2 g; Prot 3 g

LuAnn M. Johansen, Extension Youth Development Field Specialist

KOREAN SPINACH SALAD

1 cup vegetable oil
1/3 cup catsup
1 tablespoon Worcestershire sauce
3/4 cup sugar
1/4 cup white vinegar
1 pound fresh spinach
1/2 head lettuce
1 cup fresh bean sprouts
1 medium onion, thinly sliced
8 to 10 slices crisp-cooked bacon, crumbled
6 hard-cooked eggs, sliced
1 carrot, julienned
1 cup sliced fresh mushrooms

- Combine the oil, catsup, Worcestershire sauce, sugar and vinegar in a container and shake or mix well. Store, covered, in the refrigerator for 8 to 10 hours to develop the flavor.
- Tear the spinach and lettuce into bite-size pieces. Place in a large bowl. Add the remaining ingredients and mix well. Top with the dressing and toss lightly to mix.
- Yield: 12 servings.

Approx Per Serving: Cal 308; 67% Calories from Fat; T Fat 24 g; Chol 111 mg; Sod 245 mg; Carbo 19 g; Fiber 2 g; Prot 7 g

Brianna Delphey, Waukon

IOWA HERBED TOMATO SALAD

This recipe won first place in Cass County's 4-H Best of Iowa Contest.

6 tomatoes, cut into chunks
3 green bell peppers, chopped
1 cup chopped purple onion
1 cup sliced black olives
2/3 cup vegetable oil
1/4 cup vinegar
1/4 cup parsley
1/4 cup onion flakes
1 teaspoon salt
1/4 teaspoon pepper
1 teaspoon sugar
1/2 teaspoon basil
1/2 teaspoon marjoram

- Combine the tomatoes, green peppers, onion and olives in a large bowl and toss gently to mix.
- Combine the oil, vinegar, parsley, onion flakes, salt, pepper, sugar, basil and marjoram in a bowl and mix well.
- Pour the dressing over the vegetables and toss gently to mix. Chill for 3 hours before serving.
- Yield: 8 servings.

Approx Per Serving: Cal 228; 78% Calories from Fat; T Fat 21 g; Chol 0 mg; Sod 415 mg; Carbo 11 g; Fiber 3 g; Prot 2 g

Brittney Knop, Atlantic

HOT CHICKEN SALAD

2 cups chopped cooked chicken
1 (8-ounce) can water chestnuts, drained
Minced onion flakes to taste
2 cups chopped celery
1 (3-ounce) package slivered almonds
1 cup mayonnaise-type salad dressing
1/2 teaspoon salt
2 tablespoons lemon juice
1 (10-ounce) can cream of chicken soup
1/2 cup crushed potato chips

- Combine the chicken, water chestnuts, onion flakes, celery and almonds in a large bowl and mix well.
- Combine the salad dressing, salt, lemon juice and chicken soup in a bowl and mix well. Pour over the chicken salad and mix well. Pour into a 9x13-inch baking dish. Top with the potato chips.
- Bake at 350 degrees for 1 hour or until bubbly.
- Yield: 12 servings.

Approx Per Serving: Cal 212; 59% Calories from Fat; T Fat 14 g; Chol 28 mg; Sod 481 mg; Carbo 13 g; Fiber 2 g; Prot 10 g

Brooke Vestal, Emerson

TASTY TACO SALAD

Our family is always asked to bring this salad to family reunions. We also enjoy it for youth group meals and potlucks.

1 pound ground beef
1/2 onion, chopped
Salt and pepper to taste
1 (15-ounce) can kidney beans, drained
1 head lettuce, torn into bite-size pieces
2 tomatoes, chopped
8 ounces Cheddar cheese, shredded
1 (10-ounce) package taco or nacho chips, crumbled
1/2 (16-ounce) bottle Thousand Island salad dressing

- Brown the ground beef with the onion in a skillet, stirring until the ground beef is crumbly; drain. Add salt and pepper. Cool briefly. Add the kidney beans and mix well.
- Combine the lettuce, tomatoes and cheese in a large bowl and mix well. Add the ground beef mixture and mix well. Chill until serving time.
- Reserve about 1/2 cup crumbled chips. Add the remaining chips and salad dressing to the salad and mix well. Top with the reserved chips.
- Yield: 10 servings.

Approx Per Serving: Cal 462; 56% Calories from Fat; T Fat 29 g; Chol 65 mg; Sod 700 mg; Carbo 31 g; Fiber 5 g; Prot 21 g

Kiana Converse, Fredericksburg

Breads

Autumn Afternoon

by Matt Rohrig
Orient

Matt Rohrig of Adair County used the late afternoon sunlight to capture the silhouette of a fence and old telephone pole. He feels that the picture "represents our rural Iowa countryside." Matt has been enrolled in photography for five years as a member of the Orient Bulldogs 4-H Club. Matt is the son of Brian and Kathy Rohrig.

Breads • 47

SPICY LOW-FAT APPLE MUFFINS ❖

I entered these muffins at the Bremer County Fair and they went on to the Iowa State Fair.

1 cup peeled, finely chopped apples
1/4 cup sugar
1 teaspoon cinnamon
1 3/4 cups flour
1/4 cup sugar
4 teaspoons baking powder
1/2 teaspoon salt
1/2 teaspoon cinnamon
1 cup milk
1/4 cup applesauce
1 egg

- Combine the apples, 1/4 cup sugar and 1 teaspoon cinnamon in a bowl. Mix well and let stand.
- Mix the flour, 1/4 cup sugar, baking powder, salt and 1/2 teaspoon cinnamon in a bowl. Add the milk, applesauce and egg and mix well. Stir in the apples. Fill 12 greased muffin cups 3/4 full.
- Bake at 400 degrees for 25 minutes.
- Yield: 12 servings.

Approx Per Serving: Cal 129; 9% Calories from Fat; T Fat 1 g; Chol 20 mg; Sod 214 mg; Carbo 26 g; Fiber 1 g; Prot 3 g

Emilie Elsamiller, Waverly

BERRY CREAM MUFFINS

I received a blue ribbon on these muffins at the Webster County Fair.

2 cups flour
1 cup sugar
1 teaspoon baking powder
1/2 teaspoon baking soda
1/2 teaspoon salt
1 1/2 cups fresh or frozen raspberries
2 eggs, beaten
1 cup sour cream
1/2 cup vegetable oil
1/2 teaspoon vanilla extract

- Combine the flour, sugar, baking powder, baking soda and salt in a bowl and mix well. Add the berries and toss lightly to coat.
- Combine the eggs, sour cream, oil and vanilla in a bowl and mix well. Stir into the dry ingredients just until moistened. Fill greased or paper-lined muffin cups 2/3 full.
- Bake at 400 degrees for 20 to 25 minutes or until the muffins test done.
- Yield: 12 servings.

Approx Per Serving: Cal 282; 45% Calories from Fat; T Fat 14 g; Chol 44 mg; Sod 172 mg; Carbo 35 g; Fiber 1 g; Prot 4 g

Mitch Adkins, Clare

BRAN MUFFINS ❖

This is a great recipe to make ahead and have on hand for unexpected guests or a quick meal. It also makes a nice gift. I modified to make it "heart healthy" and won a purple ribbon at the Hamilton County Fair.

3 cups sugar
5 cups flour
5 teaspoons baking soda
1 teaspoon salt
1 (15-ounce) package raisin bran
8 egg whites or equivalent egg substitute
½ cup canola oil
½ cup applesauce
1 quart low-fat buttermilk

- Combine the first 5 ingredients in a very large bowl and mix well.
- Beat the egg whites in a bowl until foamy. Add the egg whites and remaining ingredients to the dry ingredients, stirring just until combined. Store in airtight containers in the refrigerator for 4 hours or longer before using.
- Do not stir. Spoon about ⅓ cup mixture into each greased muffin cup.
- Bake at 375 degrees for 15 minutes or until the muffins test done.
- Yield: 60 servings.

Approx Per Serving: Cal 126; 15% Calories from Fat; T Fat 2 g; Chol 1 mg; Sod 178 mg; Carbo 25 g; Fiber 1 g; Prot 3 g

Nancy Stribe, Webster City

RHUBARB OR APPLE MUFFINS

I found this recipe in a magazine and tried them for the county fair. We make them often now.

1¼ cups packed brown sugar
½ cup vegetable oil
1 egg
2 teaspoons vanilla extract
1 cup buttermilk
½ cup chopped walnuts
1½ cups finely chopped rhubarb or apples
2½ cups flour
1 teaspoon baking soda
1 teaspoon baking powder
1 teaspoon salt
1 tablespoon melted margarine
⅓ cup sugar
2 teaspoons cinnamon

- Combine the brown sugar and oil in a bowl and mix well. Add the egg, vanilla and buttermilk and mix well. Stir in the walnuts and rhubarb.
- Mix the next 4 ingredients in a bowl. Add to the rhubarb mixture. Fill greased and floured or paper-lined muffin cups ¾ full.
- Mix the margarine, sugar and cinnamon in a bowl. Sprinkle over the muffins.
- Bake at 350 degrees for 20 to 25 minutes or until the muffins test done.
- Yield: 20 servings.

Approx Per Serving: Cal 197; 38% Calories from Fat; T Fat 8 g; Chol 11 mg; Sod 192 mg; Carbo 28 g; Fiber 1 g; Prot 3 g

Melissa Allen, Promise City

BANANA BREAD

I made this for the fair this year and won a blue ribbon. This is the first recipe I've ever made all on my own.

3/4 cup margarine
1 1/2 cups sugar
2 eggs, beaten
3 cups flour
2 teaspoons baking powder
1/2 teaspoon salt
1/2 teaspoon baking soda
1/4 cup milk
3/4 cup mashed bananas

- Cream the margarine and sugar in a mixer bowl until light and fluffy. Blend in the eggs.
- Mix the dry ingredients together in a bowl. Mix the milk and bananas in a bowl. Add the dry ingredients and bananas alternately to the creamed mixture, beating constantly. Pour into 2 greased 5x9-inch loaf pans.
- Bake at 350 degrees for 40 to 45 minutes or until the bread tests done.
- Yield: 15 servings.

Approx Per Serving: Cal 273; 33% Calories from Fat; T Fat 10 g; Chol 29 mg; Sod 261 mg; Carbo 42 g; Fiber 1 g; Prot 4 g

Angie Lytle, Harlan

CINNAMON LOAF ❖

1/4 cup margarine
1 cup sugar
1 egg
1 teaspoon baking soda
2 cups flour
1 cup buttermilk
1/3 cup sugar
1 teaspoon cinnamon

- Cream the margarine and 1 cup sugar in a mixer bowl until light and fluffy. Add the egg and mix well.
- Mix the baking soda and flour together. Add to the creamed mixture alternately with the buttermilk, beating constantly.
- Spoon 1/3 of the batter into a buttered 5x9-inch loaf pan. Layer a mixture of 1/3 cup sugar and cinnamon and remaining batter 1/2 at a time in the prepared pan. Cut through the layers roughly 2 or 3 times with a knife to marbelize.
- Bake at 350 degrees for 40 to 45 minutes or until the bread tests done. Invert onto wire racks to cool.
- Yield: 12 servings.

Approx Per Serving: Cal 210; 20% Calories from Fat; T Fat 5 g; Chol 18 mg; Sod 140 mg; Carbo 39 g; Fiber 1 g; Prot 3 g

Rachel Ochsendorf, Boyden

MOIST AND SPICY PUMPKIN BREAD ❖

This recipe has been a favorite for over twenty-five years in our family.

1 cup packed brown sugar
½ cup sugar
1 cup cooked pumpkin
½ cup vegetable oil
2 eggs
2 cups flour
1 teaspoon baking soda
½ teaspoon salt
½ teaspoon nutmeg
½ teaspoon ginger
1 teaspoon cinnamon
1 cup raisins or pecans
¼ cup water

- Combine the brown sugar, sugar, pumpkin, oil and eggs in a bowl and mix well.
- Sift the flour, baking soda, salt and spices together. Add to the pumpkin mixture. Stir in the raisins and water. Pour into 2 greased and floured 5x9-inch loaf pans.
- Bake at 350 degrees for 1 hour and 5 minutes or until the bread tests done. Invert onto wire racks to cool.
- Yield: 24 servings.

Approx Per Serving: Cal 151; 30% Calories from Fat; T Fat 5 g; Chol 18 mg; Sod 88 mg; Carbo 25 g; Fiber 1 g; Prot 2 g

Christa Sindt, Story City

PUMPKIN BREAD

I received a blue ribbon on this recipe at the Jones County Fair.

3 cups sugar
3⅓ cups flour
2 teaspoons baking soda
1½ teaspoons salt
1 teaspoon cinnamon
1 teaspoon nutmeg
1 cup vegetable oil
4 eggs
⅓ cup water
2 cups canned pumpkin

- Sift the sugar, flour, baking soda, salt and spices into a bowl. Make a well in the center. Add the remaining ingredients and mix well. Pour into 2 greased and floured 5x9-inch loaf pans.
- Bake at 350 degrees for 1 hour or until the bread tests done. Invert onto wire racks to cool.
- Yield: 24 servings.

Approx Per Serving: Cal 260; 35% Calories from Fat; T Fat 10 g; Chol 35 mg; Sod 214 mg; Carbo 40 g; Fiber 1 g; Prot 3 g

Rachel Stolte, Olin

THE BEST RHUBARB BREAD

Given to me by Carol McGarvey and her daughter, Molly. Carol is Food Editor of the Des Moines Register.

1½ cups packed brown sugar
1 egg
⅔ cup vegetable oil
1 teaspoon vanilla extract
1 cup buttermilk
2½ cups flour
1 teaspoon salt
1 teaspoon baking soda
2 cups 1-inch fresh or frozen rhubarb pieces
½ cup chopped pecans
½ cup sugar
1 tablespoon margarine, softened
½ teaspoon cinnamon

- Combine the brown sugar, egg, oil, vanilla and buttermilk in a bowl and mix well.
- Sift the flour, salt and baking soda together. Add to the brown sugar mixture. Fold in the rhubarb and pecans. Pour into 2 greased 5x9-inch loaf pans. Sprinkle with a mixture of sugar, margarine and cinnamon.
- Bake at 350 degrees for 1 hour or until the bread tests done. Cool in the pans. Invert onto wire racks.
- Yield: 24 servings.

Approx Per Serving: Cal 181; 42% Calories from Fat; T Fat 9 g; Chol 9 mg; Sod 146 mg; Carbo 24 g; Fiber 1 g; Prot 2 g

Arlette J. Hollister, West Des Moines

FRY BREAD

4 cups flour
4 teaspoons baking powder
1 teaspoon salt
2 tablespoons vegetable oil
1 cup water
Vegetable oil for frying

- Combine the flour, baking powder and salt in a bowl and mix well. Add 2 tablespoons oil and water and mix well.
- Knead the dough with floured hands until elastic but not sticky. Shape into plum-size balls; flatten and stretch until shaped like a thin pancake.
- Roll on a lightly floured surface until very flat. Punch a hole in the center.
- Fry the bread in 2 inches of hot oil until brown, turning once.
- Serve topped with confectioners' sugar, honey or salsa.
- Yield: 5 servings.

Approx Per Serving: Cal 416; 14% Calories from Fat; T Fat 6 g; Chol 0 mg; Sod 691 mg; Carbo 77 g; Fiber 3 g; Prot 10 g
Nutritional information does not include oil for frying.

Christina Vik, George

SWEDISH PANCAKES ❖

Cathy Backstrom was the best babysitter in the world! She took care of my family for eleven years. She made great breakfasts and her Swedish pancakes were my favorites.

3 eggs
2 tablespoons sugar
1 cup milk
¾ cup flour

- Beat the eggs in a bowl. Add the sugar, milk and flour. Beat with a fork until smooth.
- Heat a griddle sprayed with nonstick cooking spray. Pour a small circle of batter in the center and tilt the griddle until the batter is flat like a crepe. Bake until light brown, turning once. Repeat with the remaining batter.
- Roll the pancakes up and serve with butter and syrup.
- Yield: 6 servings.

Approx Per Serving: Cal 135; 27% Calories from Fat; T Fat 4 g; Chol 112 mg; Sod 52 mg; Carbo 18 g; Fiber <1 g; Prot 6 g

Emily Baade, Havelock

MONKEY BREAD

These are fun to make.

3 (7-ounce) cans refrigerator rolls
½ cup packed brown sugar
¼ cup melted butter or margarine
½ teaspoon cinnamon

- Cut the rolls into quarters and place in a microwave bundt pan. Stir the brown sugar, butter and cinnamon in a bowl and pour over the cut rolls.
- Microwave using the manufacturer's instructions until brown. Invert onto a serving plate.
- Yield: 15 servings.

Approx Per Serving: Cal 209; 42% Calories from Fat; T Fat 11 g; Chol 8 mg; Sod 629 mg; Carbo 30 g; Fiber 0 g; Prot 4 g

Meredith Geschke, New Hampton

---

*Brianne Barrick, Wapello, makes a **Butter Frosting** by combining 3 tablespoons softened butter, 2¼ cups confectioners' sugar and 1 teaspoon vanilla extract in a bowl. Add 2 to 4 tablespoons milk to make of spreading consistency. Spread on scones, muffins, bread, or cake.*

ORANGE POPPY SEED SCONES

These are great for brunch or a luncheon.

2 1/4 cups flour
1/2 cup sugar
1/4 cup poppy seeds
1 teaspoon cream of tartar
3/4 teaspoon baking soda
1/2 teaspoon salt
1/2 cup butter
1/4 cup orange juice
1 egg
1/4 teaspoon orange peel
1 egg white
1/2 teaspoon water

- Mix the first 6 ingredients in a bowl. Cut in the butter until crumbly.
- Mix the orange juice, egg and orange peel in a bowl and add to the flour mixture, mixing well. The dough will be sticky.
- Place the dough in the center of a greased baking sheet. Pat with floured hands into a 9-inch circle. Brush with a mixture of the egg white and water. Cut into 8 wedges with a serrated knife.
- Bake at 375 degrees for 20 to 25 minutes or until light brown. Cool on a wire rack.
- Yield: 8 servings.

Approx Per Serving: Cal 317; 41% Calories from Fat; T Fat 15 g; Chol 58 mg; Sod 344 mg; Carbo 42 g; Fiber 2 g; Prot 6 g

Whitney Bean, West Des Moines

BUBBLE BREAD

2 loaves frozen bread dough, thawed
1 (4-ounce) package butterscotch pudding and pie filling mix
1 cup packed brown sugar
1/2 cup melted butter
1 teaspoon cinnamon
1 teaspoon vanilla extract
1/2 cup milk

- Cut the bread dough into cubes and place in a buttered 9x13-inch baking dish.
- Combine the remaining ingredients in a bowl and mix well. Pour over the dough. Let rise, using the roll package directions.
- Bake at 350 degrees for 25 to 30 minutes or until light brown.
- Do not use instant pudding in this recipe.
- Yield: 12 servings.

Approx Per Serving: Cal 363; 27% Calories from Fat; T Fat 11 g; Chol 22 mg; Sod 562 mg; Carbo 60 g; Fiber 2 g; Prot 7 g

Valery Sue Rahe, Dyersville

CREAM CHEESE COFFEE CAKE

This can be made the night before it is needed and reheated in the microwave.

1 loaf frozen bread dough, thawed
8 ounces cream cheese, softened
1/2 cup sugar
1 egg, beaten
1 teaspoon vanilla extract
6 tablespoons margarine or butter
1/2 cup sugar
3/4 cup flour
1 cup confectioners' sugar
1 tablespoon milk

- Roll the dough into a circle on a floured surface. Place on a 12-inch baking pan.
- Beat the cream cheese and 1/2 cup sugar in a bowl. Add the egg and vanilla and beat until smooth. Spread over the dough.
- Cut the margarine into a mixture of 1/2 cup sugar and flour in a bowl until crumbly. Sprinkle over the cream cheese mixture. Let rise using the package directions for 30 minutes.
- Bake at 375 degrees for 30 minutes.
- Mix the confectioners' sugar and milk in a bowl until smooth. Drizzle over the hot coffee cake.
- Yield: 8 servings.

Approx Per Serving: Cal 535; 36% Calories from Fat; T Fat 22 g; Chol 58 mg; Sod 459 mg; Carbo 77 g; Fiber 2 g; Prot 9 g

Tara Leusink, Hull

JIFFY ALMOND PAN PIZZA

I made this as a presentation and took it on to our county level. I was a Junior member at the time and could go no further with it. I also won at the county and state levels in the Milk Made Magic Contest.

1 loaf frozen bread dough, thawed
8 ounces cream cheese, softened
1/2 cup sugar
1 egg
1 teaspoon almond extract
6 tablespoons butter
1/2 cup sugar
3/4 cup flour
1/2 cup sliced almonds
1/4 cup shredded coconut, or to taste

- Spread the dough onto a greased 12-inch baking pan.
- Mix the cream cheese, 1/2 cup sugar, egg and almond extract in a bowl. Spread over the dough.
- Cut the butter into a mixture of 1/2 cup sugar and flour in a bowl until a soft ball forms. Crumble over the cream cheese mixture. Top with the almonds and coconut.
- Bake at 375 degrees for 20 to 30 minutes or until brown. May drizzle with frosting while warm.
- Yield: 8 servings.

Approx Per Serving: Cal 521; 43% Calories from Fat; T Fat 25 g; Chol 81 mg; Sod 446 mg; Carbo 65 g; Fiber 3 g; Prot 10 g

Jill Leistikow, Readlyn

PEPPERONI BREAD

1 loaf frozen bread dough, thawed
36 to 40 slices pepperoni
2/3 cup shredded mozzarella cheese
1/3 cup shredded Cheddar cheese
2 eggs, beaten
1/3 cup grated Parmesan cheese
1 egg white, beaten

- Roll the dough into a large rectangle on a floured surface. Sprinkle with the pepperoni, mozzarella cheese and Cheddar cheese.
- Mix the eggs and Parmesan cheese in a bowl. Spread over the cheese layer. Roll as for a jelly roll to enclose the filling. Place on a lightly greased baking sheet.
- Bake at 375 degrees for 20 minutes. Brush with the egg white. Bake for 5 to 10 minutes longer or until brown. Cut into 1-inch slices.
- Yield: 24 servings.

Approx Per Serving: Cal 124; 50% Calories from Fat; T Fat 7 g; Chol 30 mg; Sod 330 mg; Carbo 10 g; Fiber 1 g; Prot 6 g

Jessi Kleitsch, Readlyn

CARAMEL NUT ROLLS IN A BREAD MACHINE

11 tablespoons milk
3 eggs
4 cups bread flour
1 teaspoon salt
1/2 cup sugar
1/2 cup butter
1 teaspoon vanilla extract
1 tablespoon dry yeast
1/2 cup melted margarine
3/4 cup packed brown sugar
1/2 cup chopped pecans
1/4 cup margarine, softened
1/4 cup sugar
1 teaspoon cinnamon

- Place the first 8 ingredients in the bread machine pan. Use the dough cycle according to the manufacturer's instructions.
- Combine 1/2 cup melted margarine and brown sugar in a bowl. Spread in a 9x13-inch baking dish. Sprinkle with the pecans.
- Remove the dough when the cycle is finished and place on a floured surface. Roll into a large rectangle. Spread 1/4 cup margarine over the surface. Sprinkle a mixture of 1/4 cup sugar and cinnamon over the dough. Roll as for a jelly roll, pressing the seam closed. Cut the roll into 12 slices and place seamside down in the prepared baking dish. Let rise until doubled in bulk.
- Bake at 350 degrees for 20 minutes or until golden brown. Invert onto a serving tray so the caramel drains over the rolls.
- Yield: 12 servings.

Approx Per Serving: Cal 475; 46% Calories from Fat; T Fat 25 g; Chol 76 mg; Sod 418 mg; Carbo 57 g; Fiber 2 g; Prot 7 g

Autumn Griffieon, Ankeny

CARROT-DILL BREAD IN A BREAD MACHINE ❖

This received Junior Recognition at the 1996 Kossuth County Fair.

1 cup plus 2 tablespoons water
½ cup shredded carrot
2 tablespoons margarine
2 tablespoons sugar
3 cups bread flour
1 cup fiberous cereal
1½ teaspoons dried dillweed
1 teaspoon salt
1 teaspoon dry yeast

- Place all the ingredients in the bread machine using the manufacturer's instructions. Measure carefully.
- Select the Basic White cycle.
- Remove the baked bread and place on a wire rack to cool.
- Yield: 12 servings.

Approx Per Serving: Cal 160; 14% Calories from Fat; T Fat 2 g; Chol 0 mg; Sod 242 mg; Carbo 30 g; Fiber 3 g; Prot 4 g

Aaron Kent, Algona

OATMEAL BREAD IN A BREAD MACHINE ❖

This used to be my grandmother's recipe and a favorite of the family. I changed it to use in the bread machine. It has won a State Fair Entry on the county level and a blue ribbon at the State Fair.

¾ cup quick rolled oats
⅓ cup plus 1 tablespoon whole wheat flour
⅓ cup packed brown sugar
½ tablespoon salt
1½ tablespoons margarine
1½ cups warm water
3½ cups bread flour
1 package dry yeast

- Pour all the ingredients into the bread machine using the manufacturer's instructions. I always bake it on the light color.
- Remove the baked bread to a wire rack to cool.
- Yield: 12 servings.

Approx Per Serving: Cal 198; 10% Calories from Fat; T Fat 2 g; Chol 0 mg; Sod 286 mg; Carbo 39 g; Fiber 2 g; Prot 5 g

Brett Lindner, Keokuk

Breads • 57

COFFEE CAN WHEAT BREAD ❖

This bread recipe was given to me by my grandmother. It won Grand Champion at the Woodbury County Fair and a blue ribbon at State Fair. It is very easy and exciting to wait for the lids to pop off.

1 package dry yeast
1/2 cup warm water
1 tablespoon sugar
1 teaspoon salt
3 cups all-purpose flour
1 cup whole wheat flour
1 (12-ounce) can evaporated milk

- Dissolve the yeast in the warm water. Stir in the sugar and salt. Combine the yeast mixture, all-purpose flour, whole wheat flour and evaporated milk in a bowl and mix well. Spoon into 2 greased 1-pound coffee cans. Cover with the greased lids.
- Let rise in a warm place until the lids pop off.
- The ISU Family Nutrition and Health Specialist recommends baking in 2 greased loaf pans. Cover with greased waxed paper. Let rise in a warm place until the dough pushes the waxed paper above the rim of the pans. Remove the waxed paper.
- Bake at 400 degrees for 35 minutes.
- Yield: 24 servings.

Approx Per Serving: Cal 96; 13% Calories from Fat; T Fat 1 g; Chol 4 mg; Sod 105 mg; Carbo 18 g; Fiber 1 g; Prot 3 g

Angie Pithan, Anthon

CHEESE SNACK BREAD

This is served at Camp Aldersgate in Villisca, Iowa, where I attended camp and am now a counselor. It's great with spaghetti.

1 package dry yeast
1 tablespoon sugar
1/4 cup warm water
3/4 cup milk
1/4 cup butter
1 teaspoon salt
3 to 3 1/2 cups flour
2 cups shredded Cheddar cheese
5 tablespoons milk
1 egg
1 tablespoon minced onion

- Dissolve the yeast and sugar in the water in a glass measure. Combine 3/4 cup milk, butter and salt in a saucepan. Heat to 105 to 115 degrees, stirring until the butter melts.
- Combine the yeast mixture, milk mixture and 3 cups flour in a large bowl and mix well. Add the remaining flour as needed to make a soft dough. Knead for 3 minutes. Place in a greased bowl, turning to grease the surface.
- Let rise, covered, for 30 to 45 minutes or until doubled in bulk. Punch down the dough and pat out on a greased 11x15-inch baking pan. Let rise, covered, for 30 minutes.
- Mix the cheese, 5 tablespoons milk, egg and minced onion in a bowl. Spread over the dough.
- Bake at 375 degrees for 20 minutes. Cool slightly and cut into squares.
- Yield: 24 servings.

Approx Per Serving: Cal 134; 39% Calories from Fat; T Fat 6 g; Chol 25 mg; Sod 175 mg; Carbo 15 g; Fiber 1 g; Prot 5 g

Kathy Summy, Crescent

MARBLE SWIRL BREAD

A fun bread to bake and very tasty. Received Grand Champion at my County Fair.

2 3/4 to 3 1/4 cups all-purpose flour
1/4 cup sugar
1 package dry yeast
1 teaspoon salt
1 1/3 cups water
1/4 cup butter or margarine
1 egg
2 tablespoons molasses
2 teaspoons baking cocoa
1 teaspoon instant coffee
1 to 1 1/4 cups rye flour
1 tablespoon water
1 egg yolk

- Combine 1 1/2 cups of the all-purpose flour, sugar, yeast and salt in a large mixer bowl.
- Combine 1 1/3 cups water and butter in a saucepan. Heat over low heat to 120 to 130 degrees. Beat at low speed into the flour mixture. Beat at medium speed for 2 minutes. Beat in the egg and 1/2 cup of the all-purpose flour at low speed. Beat at medium speed for 2 minutes.
- Reserve half the batter (about 1 1/3 cups) in a bowl. Stir 3/4 cup of the all-purpose flour into the remaining batter to make a stiff dough, adding the remaining 1/2 cup all-purpose flour if necessary.
- Stir the molasses, cocoa and coffee powder into the reserved batter. Add enough rye flour to make a stiff dough.
- Cover both bowls. Let rise in a warm place for 1 hour or until doubled in bulk.
- Punch down both doughs. Knead each on a floured surface for 1 minute. Let rise, covered with a towel, for 10 minutes.
- Roll the lighter dough into a 9x12-inch rectangle. Roll the darker dough into an 8x12-inch rectangle. Place on top of the light dough. Roll as for a jelly roll from the long side, pressing seam and ends to seal. Place seamside down on a greased 10x15-inch baking sheet, tucking the ends under. Let rise, covered with a towel, in a warm place for 45 minutes or until doubled in bulk.
- Mix 1 tablespoon water and egg yolk in a bowl. Cut three 1/2-inch-deep slashes across the top of dough with a sharp knife. Brush with the egg wash.
- Bake at 350 degrees for 35 to 40 minutes or until the loaf is brown and sounds hollow when tapped. Remove from the baking sheet to a wire rack to cool.
- Yield: 12 servings.

Approx Per Serving: Cal 234; 20% Calories from Fat; T Fat 5 g; Chol 46 mg; Sod 225 mg; Carbo 41 g; Fiber 3 g; Prot 6 g

Jami Sieger, Hornick

Breads • 59

PIONEER WHITE BREAD ❖

I used this recipe for a food and nutrition project which was selected for the 1996 State Fair.

2½ to 3 cups flour
1 package dry yeast
1¼ cups water
1 tablespoon sugar
¾ teaspoon salt
2 tablespoons cornmeal

- Combine 1 cup of the flour and yeast in a large mixer bowl.
- Heat the water, sugar and salt in a saucepan to 115 to 120 degrees, stirring to dissolve the sugar. Add to the dry mixture and beat for 3 minutes. Stir in enough of the remaining flour to make a soft dough. Shape into a ball and place in a greased bowl, turning to coat the surface. Let rise, covered, for 1 hour or until doubled in bulk. Punch down the dough. Let rise, covered, for 10 minutes.
- Grease a 1-quart baking dish; sprinkle with cornmeal. Place the dough in the prepared baking dish. Let rise, covered, for 30 to 45 minutes or until doubled in bulk.
- Bake at 400 degrees for 40 to 45 minutes. Remove to a wire rack to cool.
- Yield: 12 servings.

Approx Per Serving: Cal 125; 3% Calories from Fat; T Fat <1 g; Chol 0 mg; Sod 134 mg; Carbo 26 g; Fiber 1 g; Prot 4 g

Kerry McDonald, Preston

WHITE BREAD ❖

We have grown up making this fast bread. It's just enough for a meal and once we learned, more-difficult breads were easier.

1 package dry yeast
1 cup hot (110 degrees) water
2 tablespoons sugar
2 tablespoons melted butter
1 teaspoon salt
3 cups flour

- Dissolve the yeast in the hot water in a large bowl. Stir in the sugar, butter and salt. Add 2 cups of the flour 1 cup at a time, mixing well after each addition. Mix in the remaining 1 cup flour with hands. Knead the dough for about 5 minutes. Shape into a loaf. Place in a greased 5x9-inch loaf pan. Let rise, covered with a damp cloth, in a warm place for 30 to 45 minutes or until doubled in bulk.
- Bake at 375 degrees for 20 to 30 minutes or until brown. Remove to a wire rack to cool.
- This is also good to use for pizza dough and cinnamon rolls. For variety in flavor, substitute 1 cup flour with any other flour.
- Yield: 12 servings.

Approx Per Serving: Cal 140; 15% Calories from Fat; T Fat 2 g; Chol 5 mg; Sod 198 mg; Carbo 26 g; Fiber 1 g; Prot 3 g

Jessica, Andrea, Lyle and August McIntosh, Dunkerton

SHAMBAUGH'S PRIZE BREAD ❖

I'm sure this is nearly identical to the bread my mother made when I was growing up, only she didn't follow an exact recipe, just "knew it by heart."

1 cup milk
3 tablespoons honey
2 teaspoons salt
1/4 cup butter, margarine or vegetable oil
2 packages dry yeast
1 1/4 cups warm (105 to 115 degrees) water
6 1/2 to 7 cups unbleached white flour
2 tablespoons melted butter

- Bring the milk just to a simmer in a saucepan. Add the honey, salt and 1/4 cup butter. Cool to lukewarm (110 to 115 degrees).
- Dissolve the yeast in the warm water in a large bowl. Add the milk mixture, mixing well. Add half the flour, beating for 5 minutes or until smooth. Add the remaining flour gradually, mixing well.
- Knead on a floured surface for 10 minutes or until smooth and elastic. Place in an oiled bowl, turning to grease the surface. Let rise, covered, in a warm (85 degrees) place for 1 hour or until doubled in bulk.
- Punch down the dough. Divide into halves on a floured surface. Shape into loaves and place in 2 oiled 4x8-inch loaf pans. Brush tops with melted butter. Let rise, covered, for 1 hour or until doubled in bulk.
- Bake at 375 degrees for 40 to 45 minutes or until the bread tests done. Remove to wire racks to cool.
- Yield: 24 servings.

Approx Per Serving: Cal 158; 23% Calories from Fat; T Fat 4 g; Chol 8 mg; Sod 213 mg; Carbo 27 g; Fiber <1 g; Prot 4 g

Ruth Shambaugh Watkins, daughter of Ira and Jessie Field Shambaugh, Clarinda

BROOKLYN BAGELS ❖

I went to the State Fair in 1996 and received a participation ribbon. I did a nutritional analysis and cost per serving.

1 package dry yeast
2 tablespoons honey
1 1/2 cups warm water
2 teaspoons salt
4 to 5 cups flour
1 egg white
1 teaspoon water

- Dissolve the yeast in a mixture of honey and 1 1/2 cups water in a bowl. Mix in the salt and flour. Knead until smooth. Let rest for 15 minutes. Divide the dough into 12 portions. Shape each into a ball and make a hole in the center with your thumb until the bagel is 2 inches in diameter. Let rise for 20 to 30 minutes.
- Drop the bagels into a large stockpot of boiling water. Simmer for 7 minutes after the bagels rise to the top. Place on a greased 10x15-inch baking pan.
- Beat the egg white and 1 teaspoon water in a bowl. Brush the bagels with the egg wash.
- Bake at 375 degrees for 25 minutes for chewy bagels or for 30 minutes for crispy bagels.
- Yield: 12 servings.

Approx Per Serving: Cal 203; 2% Calories from Fat; T Fat 1 g; Chol 0 mg; Sod 361 mg; Carbo 43 g; Fiber 2 g; Prot 6 g

Jessica Rohrig, Orient

Breads • 61

FINNISH BREAD ❖

This is the traditional bread in Finland. It received Merit at Woodbury County Fair.

1 package dry yeast
2 cups warm (110 to 115 degrees) water
1 cup whole wheat flour
2 tablespoons melted margarine
1 tablespoon brown sugar
2 teaspoons salt
4½ to 5 cups flour
2 tablespoons melted margarine

- Dissolve the yeast in the water in a large bowl. Add the whole wheat flour, 2 tablespoons margarine, brown sugar, salt and 2 cups of the flour. Beat until smooth. Add enough of the remaining flour to form a soft dough. Knead on a floured surface for 6 to 8 minutes or until smooth and elastic. Place in a greased bowl, turning to grease the surface. Let rise, covered, in a warm place for 1 hour or until doubled in bulk.
- Punch down the dough. Shape into two 6-inch rounds. Place on a greased baking sheet. Cut slashes in the tops with a knife. Let rise, covered, for 40 minutes or until doubled in bulk.
- Bake at 400 degrees for 40 to 45 minutes or until golden brown. Brush the tops with the remaining 2 tablespoons margarine.
- Yield: 24 servings.

Approx Per Serving: Cal 131; 16% Calories from Fat; T Fat 2 g; Chol 0 mg; Sod 201 mg; Carbo 24 g; Fiber 1 g; Prot 4 g

Jami Sieger, Hornick

KOLACHES

This recipe was handed down to our family by a cousin, Stella Mallie, who was well known for her baking and especially her kolaches.

3 cups lukewarm milk
2 packages dry yeast
½ cup sugar
3 to 6 cups flour
4 egg yolks
1 tablespoon salt
½ cup vegetable oil
2 tablespoons vegetable oil
2 cups fruit filling

- Combine the milk, yeast and sugar in a bowl, stirring until the yeast dissolves. Stir in 3 cups of the flour. Let stand for 10 minutes.
- Add the egg yolks, salt, ½ cup oil and enough of the remaining flour to make a soft dough. Stir until smooth and glossy. Let rise for 1 hour or until doubled in bulk.
- Shape into balls. Place on a greased baking sheet and brush lightly with 2 tablespoons oil. Let rise. Make an indention in the center of each and add a filling of chopped fruit or jam. Let rise again.
- Bake at 425 degrees for 10 to 15 minutes or until light brown.
- Yield: 36 servings.

Approx Per Serving: Cal 127; 35% Calories from Fat; T Fat 5 g; Chol 24 mg; Sod 179 mg; Carbo 19 g; Fiber 1 g; Prot 3 g
Nutritional information does not include fruit filling.

Bruce Mallie, Tripoli

POTATO REFRIGERATOR ROLLS

1 package dry yeast
1½ cups warm water
⅔ cup sugar
1½ teaspoons salt
⅔ cup shortening
2 eggs
1 cup lukewarm mashed potatoes
7 to 7½ cups flour

- Dissolve the yeast in the water in a large bowl. Add the sugar, salt, shortening, eggs, mashed potatoes and 4 cups of the flour. Beat until smooth. Add enough of the remaining flour to make a soft dough.
- Turn dough onto a floured surface. Knead for 5 minutes or until smooth. Shape into a ball and place in a greased bowl, turning to grease the surface. Chill, tightly covered, for at least 8 hours.
- Divide the dough into 2 portions 2 to 2½ hours before serving. Roll each portion on a floured surface. Cut into rolls. Place on a greased baking sheet. Let rise until doubled in bulk.
- Bake at 400 degrees for 10 minutes or until light brown.
- May shape dough into small dinner rolls, large hamburger buns or into ovals for hotdog buns.
- Yield: 24 servings.

Approx Per Serving: Cal 228; 26% Calories from Fat; T Fat 7 g; Chol 18 mg; Sod 166 mg; Carbo 37 g; Fiber 1 g; Prot 5 g

Tammy Chapman, Hawarden

SEVENTY-FIVE-MINUTE ROLLS

This quick recipe is a family favorite. It is easy for a 4-H'er's first yeast bread.

1 cup milk
½ cup water
¼ cup margarine
2 cups whole wheat flour
3 tablespoons sugar
1 teaspoon salt
2 packages dry yeast
2 to 2½ cups all-purpose flour
½ cup melted margarine

- Combine the milk, water and ¼ cup margarine in a saucepan. Heat to 120 to 130 degrees.
- Combine the whole wheat flour, sugar, salt and yeast in a bowl and mix well. Add the milk mixture and mix well. Add enough of the all-purpose flour to make a soft dough. Turn onto a floured surface and knead for 5 minutes. Shape into a ball. Place in a greased bowl, turning to grease the surface.
- Place the bowl in a pan of 100-degree water. Cover and let stand for 15 minutes.
- Turn onto a floured surface. Divide into 2 portions. Roll each into a circle ¼-inch thick. Brush with some of the melted margarine. Cut into quarters. Cut each quarter into pie-shaped thirds. Roll from the wide end. Place with the tip underneath on a greased baking sheet. Let rise, covered, for 15 minutes in a 100-degree oven with a pan of hot water.
- Bake at 375 degrees for 12 to 15 minutes. Brush with the remaining margarine.
- Yield: 24 servings.

Approx Per Serving: Cal 146; 39% Calories from Fat; T Fat 6 g; Chol 1 mg; Sod 162 mg; Carbo 20 g; Fiber 2 g; Prot 3 g

Richard Abbott, Webster City

Vegetables, Side Dishes, and Accompaniments

Bridge at Pine Lake in Eldora

by Michael Moeller
Holland

Springtime in Iowa, a favorite season for photographer Michael Moeller who shot this photo on a family trip to Eldora. Michael is a member of the Colfax Future Farmers 4-H Club in Grundy County, and this is his fourth year in the photography project. Michael is the son of Jerry and Glenda Moeller.

Vegetables • 65

CURRIED BEANS ❖

2 slices bacon, chopped
½ cup chopped onion
1 apple, chopped
1 green bell pepper, chopped
2 (16-ounce) cans red beans, drained
1 (16-ounce) can chopped tomatoes
½ cup packed brown sugar
1½ teaspoons curry powder
Salt and pepper to taste
½ cup grated Parmesan cheese

- Sauté the bacon with the onion, apple and green pepper in a large skillet until crisp; drain. Add the red beans, tomatoes, brown sugar, curry powder, salt and pepper and mix well. Pour into a 1-quart baking dish. Let stand, covered, in the refrigerator for several hours.
- Sprinkle with the Parmesan cheese.
- Bake at 350 degrees for 1 hour.
- Yield: 16 servings.

Approx Per Serving: Cal 101; 14% Calories from Fat; T Fat 2 g; Chol 3 mg; Sod 313 mg; Carbo 18 g; Fiber 4 g; Prot 5 g

Lynne Rechterman, Tipton

HARVARD BEETS ❖

1 (15-ounce) can beets
1 tablespoon cornstarch
1 tablespoon sugar
¾ teaspoon salt
Pepper to taste
¼ cup vinegar

- Drain the beets, reserving the liquid. Add enough water to the reserved liquid to measure ⅔ cup.
- Combine the cornstarch, sugar, salt and pepper in a saucepan and mix well. Add the vinegar and ⅔ cup beet liquid and water and mix well. Bring to a boil over medium heat, stirring constantly. Cook for 1 minute, stirring constantly. Stir in the beets and heat to serving temperature.
- Yield: 4 servings.

Approx Per Serving: Cal 53; 1% Calories from Fat; T Fat <1 g; Chol 0 mg; Sod 679 mg; Carbo 13 g; Fiber 1 g; Prot 1 g

Craig Rodas, Farmersburg

BROCCOLI CASSEROLE

2 (10-ounce) packages frozen chopped broccoli
1/4 cup chopped onion
1/4 cup butter
2 tablespoons flour
1/2 cup water
1 (8-ounce) jar Cheez Whiz
3 eggs, beaten
1/2 cup cracker crumbs
2 tablespoons butter

- Thaw and drain the broccoli.
- Sauté the onion in 1/4 cup butter in a large skillet until soft. Stir in the flour and water, blending well. Cook over low heat until thickened, stirring constantly. Stir in the Cheez Whiz, broccoli and eggs. Pour into an ungreased baking dish. Sprinkle with the cracker crumbs; dot with 2 tablespoons butter.
- Bake at 350 degrees for 30 minutes.
- Yield: 8 servings.

Approx Per Serving: Cal 238; 64% Calories from Fat; T Fat 17 g; Chol 118 mg; Sod 577 mg; Carbo 12 g; Fiber 2 g; Prot 10 g

Beverly Carstensen, Iowa 4-H Foundation Staff

BROCCOLI CHEESE CASSEROLE

1 (20-ounce) package frozen chopped broccoli
1/2 cup milk
1 (10-ounce) can cream of onion soup
1 (8-ounce) jar Cheez Whiz
1 cup uncooked quick-cooking rice
1/2 cup bread crumbs
2 tablespoons butter

- Cook the broccoli using the microwave instructions on the package; drain.
- Combine the milk, soup and Cheez Whiz in a bowl, stirring until smooth. Add the rice and fold in the broccoli. Spoon into a greased 1 1/2-quart baking dish. Sprinkle with the bread crumbs; dot with butter.
- Bake at 350 degrees for 35 minutes.
- Yield: 8 servings.

Approx Per Serving: Cal 240; 42% Calories from Fat; T Fat 11 g; Chol 30 mg; Sod 778 mg; Carbo 25 g; Fiber 3 g; Prot 10 g

Brad Tabke, Moville

Vegetables • 67

CHEESY CARROTS

1 (16-ounce) package carrots, sliced
1 small onion, chopped
2 cups shredded Cheddar cheese
2 tablespoons butter

- Combine the carrots and enough water to cover in a saucepan. Cook over medium heat until tender-crisp, stirring occasionally.
- Place $1/3$ of the carrots over the bottom of a round $1 1/2$-quart baking dish. Layer the onion, cheese and remaining carrots $1/2$ at a time over the top, ending with the carrots. Dot with the butter.
- Bake at 350 degrees for 20 minutes or until the cheese is melted.
- Yield: 4 servings.

Approx Per Serving: Cal 333; 66% Calories from Fat; T Fat 25 g; Chol 75 mg; Sod 449 mg; Carbo 14 g; Fiber 4 g; Prot 16 g

Heidi Conner, Lovilia

COPPER PENNY CARROTS

2 pounds carrots, sliced
1 small onion
$1/2$ green bell pepper
$1/2$ cup chopped celery
$1/2$ cup sugar
1 (10-ounce) can tomato soup
$1/4$ cup vegetable oil
1 teaspoon Worcestershire sauce
1 teaspoon mustard
Salt and pepper to taste

- Combine the carrots with enough water to cover in a saucepan. Cook over medium heat until tender-crisp. Drain and cool.
- Chop the onion and green pepper. Combine with the carrots and celery in a bowl and mix well. Chill, covered, for 8 to 10 hours.
- Combine the sugar, soup, oil, Worcestershire sauce, mustard, salt and pepper in a saucepan. Bring to a boil. Pour over the carrot mixture.
- Yield: 10 servings.

Approx Per Serving: Cal 152; 35% Calories from Fat; T Fat 6 g; Chol 0 mg; Sod 261 mg; Carbo 24 g; Fiber 3 g; Prot 2 g

Chuck Morris, Associate Director of Youth and 4-H

KIRSTEN'S CARROTS ❖

3 to 4 slices bacon, chopped
1 onion, chopped
2 pounds fresh carrots, sliced
1 cup water
$1/2$ cup sugar

- Sauté the bacon with the onion in a skillet until brown; drain.
- Mix the bacon and onion, carrots, water and sugar in a bowl. Pour into a baking dish.
- Bake at 350 degrees for 1 hour or until the carrots are tender.
- Yield: 8 servings.

Approx Per Serving: Cal 121; 13% Calories from Fat; T Fat 2 g; Chol 3 mg; Sod 91 mg; Carbo 25 g; Fiber 4 g; Prot 2 g

Kirsten Shaffer, Exira

CHEESE CORN

2 cups frozen corn, thawed
1 cup uncooked 1-inch pieces spaghetti
1 cup Velveeta cheese cubes
1/2 cup melted margarine
1/2 cup milk
2 tablespoons onion

- Combine the corn, spaghetti, cheese, margarine, milk and onion in a bowl and mix well. Pour into a 2-quart baking dish.
- Bake, covered, at 375 degrees for 30 minutes. Stir the mixture. Bake, uncovered, for 30 minutes longer.
- May also cook in a slow cooker on Low for 3 hours, stirring occasionally.
- Yield: 8 servings.

Approx Per Serving: Cal 256; 59% Calories from Fat; T Fat 17 g; Chol 18 mg; Sod 380 mg; Carbo 20 g; Fiber 2 g; Prot 7 g

Melanie Corrington, Cherokee

CORN FRITTERS

1 cup flour
1 1/2 teaspoons baking powder
1 teaspoon cinnamon
2 tablespoons confectioners' sugar
1/4 teaspoon salt
1/3 cup milk
1 egg, beaten
1 tablespoon melted butter
1 cup corn
1/2 cup shredded sharp Cheddar cheese
Vegetable oil for frying

- Combine the flour, baking powder, cinnamon, confectioners' sugar and salt in a bowl and mix well.
- Mix the milk, egg and butter together. Add to the dry ingredients 1/2 at a time, mixing well after each addition. Stir in the corn and cheese.
- Drop by tablespoonfuls a few at a time into hot oil in a skillet. Fry for 3 minutes and turn to brown both sides; drain. Serve hot.
- Yield: 20 servings.

Approx Per Serving: Cal 55; 33% Calories from Fat; T Fat 2 g; Chol 16 mg; Sod 81 mg; Carbo 7 g; Fiber <1 g; Prot 2 g
Nutritional information does not include oil for frying.

Christina Vik, George

Vegetables • 69

SCALLOPED CORN

¼ cup chopped onion
2 tablespoons butter or margarine
2 tablespoons flour
1 teaspoon salt
½ teaspoon paprika
¼ teaspoon dry mustard
Pepper to taste
¾ cup milk
1 (16-ounce) can whole kernel corn, drained
1 egg, lightly beaten

- Sauté the onion in the butter until clear. Blend in the flour and seasonings, mixing well. Add the milk gradually, stirring constantly. Bring to a boil over medium heat. Cook for 1 minute over low heat, stirring constantly. Remove from the heat.
- Add the corn and egg, mixing well. Pour into a 1-quart baking dish. May top with buttered crumbs.
- Bake at 350 degrees for 20 to 30 minutes or until brown and bubbly.
- May substitute 2 cups fresh corn for canned.
- Yield: 4 servings.

Approx Per Serving: Cal 208; 39% Calories from Fat; T Fat 10 g; Chol 75 mg; Sod 995 mg; Carbo 27 g; Fiber 2 g; Prot 7 g

Lisa Moss, Bloomfield

GOOD-LUCK BLACK-EYED PEAS ❖

My family eats these on the first day of every new year. According to tradition it gives you good luck in the coming year.

1 (15-ounce) can black-eyed peas
2 tablespoons tomatillo sauce, or to taste
1 tablespoon chopped onion
¼ cup chopped cooked ham

- Combine the black-eyed peas, tomatillo sauce, onion and ham in a microwave-safe bowl and mix well.
- Microwave for 2 minutes or until of serving temperature.
- Yield: 4 servings.

Approx Per Serving: Cal 111; 19% Calories from Fat; T Fat 2 g; Chol 5 mg; Sod 484 mg; Carbo 15 g; Fiber 7 g; Prot 8 g

Laura Lutz, Ames

MEDITERRANEAN PIZZAS

Olde Broom Factory Restaurant is on the National List of Historic Places. It serves lunches, brunches, and banquets up to 300.

6 prepared individual-size pizza crusts
1 (15-ounce) can marinated artichoke hearts
12 ounces Alfredo sauce
18 fresh spinach leaves, stemmed
1 (4-ounce) can sliced mushrooms, drained
2 fresh tomatoes, chopped
24 ounces mozzarella cheese, shredded
Basil to taste

- Place the pizza crusts on baking pans. Drain the artichoke hearts and cut into slices.
- Layer each pizza crust with 2 ounces Alfredo sauce, spinach leaves, mushrooms, tomatoes and artichoke slices. Sprinkle with the cheese and basil.
- Bake at 350 degrees for 15 minutes or until the cheese is melted and pizzas are golden brown.
- Yield: 6 servings.

Approx Per Serving: Cal 999; 55% Calories from Fat; T Fat 61 g; Chol 130 mg; Sod 1673 mg; Carbo 78 g; Fiber 11 g; Prot 35 g

Olde Broom Factory Restaurant, Cedar Falls

COUNTRY POTATOES

This recipe won second place at the Allamakee County Milk Made Magic Contest.

7 or 8 potatoes, cooked
1 (10-ounce) can cream of chicken soup
½ cup butter
1½ cups shredded Cheddar cheese
1 cup sour cream
⅓ cup minced onion
1 cup cornflake crumbs
2 tablespoons melted butter

- Grate the cooked potatoes. Place in a greased 9x13-inch baking dish.
- Heat the soup with ½ cup butter in a saucepan until the butter is melted, stirring frequently. Stir in the cheese, sour cream and onion. Pour over the potatoes.
- Mix the cornflake crumbs and melted butter together. Sprinkle over the top of the potatoes.
- Bake at 350 degrees for 1 hour.
- Yield: 15 servings.

Approx Per Serving: Cal 246; 57% Calories from Fat; T Fat 16 g; Chol 41 mg; Sod 371 mg; Carbo 21 g; Fiber 1 g; Prot 6 g

Bridget Pfiffner, Harpers Ferry

Vegetables • 71

GOOD POTATOES

This recipe can be made ahead and frozen. My grandma's is really good. I love it.

8 medium cooked potatoes, chilled
1 onion, chopped
2 tablespoons margarine or butter
1/4 cup margarine
2 cups shredded Cheddar cheese
2 cups sour cream or cream
Salt and pepper to taste

- Peel and grate the potatoes. Place in a buttered 9x13-inch baking dish.
- Sauté the onion in 2 tablespoons margarine in a large skillet. Add 1/4 cup margarine and the cheese. Cook over low heat until melted, stirring constantly. Stir in the sour cream. Pour over the grated potatoes. Add the salt and pepper and toss gently to mix.
- Bake at 350 degrees for 35 to 45 minutes or until brown and bubbly.
- Yield: 10 servings.

Approx Per Serving: Cal 345; 62% Calories from Fat; T Fat 24 g; Chol 44 mg; Sod 250 mg; Carbo 24 g; Fiber 2 g; Prot 9 g

Bryce Hoben, Wapello

801 MAYTAG BLUE CHEESE POTATOES

1 1/2 pounds small red potatoes, steamed, cut into quarters
2 tablespoons clarified butter
1 clove of garlic, minced
3 ounces Maytag blue cheese
1/3 cup whipping cream
Salt and pepper to taste
1/4 cup grated Parmesan cheese

- Sauté the potatoes in the clarified butter in a 10-inch skillet over medium-high heat until the potatoes start to brown. Add the garlic, blue cheese and whipping cream.
- Cook for 5 to 8 minutes or until a thick creamy sauce is achieved, stirring frequently. Season with salt and pepper.
- Turn out onto an oven-safe serving dish. Sprinkle with Parmesan cheese.
- Cook under a hot broiler for 2 minutes or until the cheese is brown.
- Yield: 4 servings.

Approx Per Serving: Cal 409; 46% Calories from Fat; T Fat 21 g; Chol 64 mg; Sod 492 mg; Carbo 44 g; Fiber 4 g; Prot 12 g

A creation of our young talented chef, Jonathan Poor
801 Steak and Chop House, Ltd., Des Moines

Paul Shutt, Winterset, makes **Scalloped Potatoes in a Skillet** by combining 8 to 10 sliced peeled potatoes with enough water to cover in a large skillet. Cook until the potatoes are tender and drain. Add enough milk to cover the potatoes. Add cubed Velveeta cheese, salt and pepper to taste. Cook for 20 minutes or until the cheese is melted and sauce is thickened, stirring frequently.

PARTY POTATOES

2 pounds frozen hash brown potatoes
1/2 cup melted butter
1/2 cup chopped onion
1 teaspoon salt
1/4 teaspoon pepper
1 (10-ounce) can cream of chicken soup
1 cup sour cream
1 1/2 cups shredded Cheddar cheese
1 cup milk
2 cups cornflake crumbs
1/4 cup melted butter

- Thaw the potatoes. Arrange in a greased 9x13-inch baking dish.
- Combine 1/2 cup melted butter, onion, salt, pepper, soup, sour cream, cheese and milk in a bowl and mix well. Pour over the potatoes.
- Sprinkle with cornflake crumbs. Drizzle with 1/4 cup melted butter.
- Bake at 350 degrees for 1 hour.
- Yield: 12 servings.

Approx Per Serving: Cal 348; 58% Calories from Fat; T Fat 23 g; Chol 59 mg; Sod 747 mg; Carbo 29 g; Fiber 1 g; Prot 8 g

Frankie Christoffersen, Casey

PIZZA POTATOES

1 (15-ounce) can chunky tomato sauce
1 1/2 teaspoons Italian seasoning
1/2 teaspoon Sugar Twin or Sprinkle Sweet
1/4 cup grated fat-free Parmesan cheese
1 (2-ounce) can sliced mushrooms, drained
1/3 cup shredded reduced-fat Cheddar cheese
1 (2 1/2-ounce) package lean pastrami, shredded
1/2 cup shredded reduced-fat mozzarella cheese
1 (10-ounce) package frozen hash brown potatoes, thawed

- Combine the tomato sauce, Italian seasoning, Sugar Twin and Parmesan cheese in a large bowl and mix well. Stir in the mushrooms, Cheddar cheese, pastrami, mozzarella cheese and potatoes, tossing gently to mix. Pour into an 8x8-inch baking dish sprayed with nonstick olive oil-flavor cooking spray. Cover with waxed paper.
- Microwave on High for 15 minutes, turning the dish after each 5 minutes. Let the dish stand on a wire rack for 2 to 3 minutes before serving.
- Yield: 4 servings.

Approx Per Serving: Cal 207; 21% Calories from Fat; T Fat 5 g; Chol 19 mg; Sod 518 mg; Carbo 26 g; Fiber <1 g; Prot 17 g

Karen Loupee, Reasnor

Vegetables • 73

TWICE-BAKED POTATOES

One of our family favorites and its quick to make.

4 baking potatoes
½ cup butter or margarine
½ cup sour cream
½ teaspoon salt
Pepper and paprika to taste

- Pierce the potatoes and place on a paper towel in a circle 1 inch apart in the microwave.
- Microwave on High for 12 to 16 minutes. Let stand for several minutes for potatoes to soften.
- Slice tops off the potatoes and scoop out the potato pulp, reserving the shells.
- Combine the potatoes, butter, sour cream, salt, pepper and paprika in a mixer bowl and beat until smooth. Spoon the mixture into the potato shells, mounding up if necessary. Place on a microwave-safe plate.
- Microwave on High for 4 minutes.
- Yield: 4 servings.

Approx Per Serving: Cal 398; 65% Calories from Fat; T Fat 29 g; Chol 75 mg; Sod 526 mg; Carbo 32 g; Fiber 3 g; Prot 4 g

Sarah Seehusen, Pocahontas

SWEET POTATO BALLS

¼ cup butter, softened
¾ cup packed brown sugar
2 tablespoons milk
¼ teaspoon salt
½ teaspoon grated orange peel
1 cup chopped pecans
3 cups mashed cooked sweet potatoes
8 marshmallows
1 cup crushed cornflakes

- Combine the butter, brown sugar, milk, salt, orange peel, pecans and sweet potatoes in a bowl and mix well.
- Shape ¼ cup sweet potato mixture around each marshmallow, adding additional mixture as needed. Roll each ball in cornflake crumbs. Place in a buttered 9x9-inch baking dish.
- Bake at 325 degrees for 20 minutes or until brown.
- May cover with foil and freeze before baking.
- Yield: 8 servings.

Approx Per Serving: Cal 354; 40% Calories from Fat; T Fat 16 g; Chol 16 mg; Sod 243 mg; Carbo 52 g; Fiber 4 g; Prot 3 g

Sharron Gilson, State Youth and 4-H Staff

ZESTY STUFFED TOMATOES

This came from an aunt's demonstration for 4-H in the 1960s.

6 tomatoes
¼ cup chopped green bell pepper
1 small onion, minced
2 teaspoons chopped olives
½ cup chopped celery
½ cup mayonnaise
2 cups cottage cheese
¼ teaspoon Worcestershire sauce
Salt, pepper and paprika to taste

- Rinse the tomatoes; pat dry. Cut off the tops. Scoop out the center pulp and chop, reserving the tomato shells. Place the pulp in a sieve to drain.
- Mix the drained tomato pulp with the bell pepper, onion, olives, celery, mayonnaise, cottage cheese, Worcestershire sauce and seasonings in a bowl. Spoon the mixture into the tomato shells. Garnish with parsley.
- Yield: 6 servings.

Approx Per Serving: Cal 238; 67% Calories from Fat; T Fat 18 g; Chol 21 mg; Sod 439 mg; Carbo 10 g; Fiber 2 g; Prot 10 g

Monica Studer, Wesley

VEGETABLE CASSEROLE

This recipe holds well for a covered-dish dinner.

2 (10-ounce) packages frozen mixed vegetables
1 (10-ounce) can cream of celery soup
1 (10-ounce) can Cheddar cheese soup
Salt and pepper to taste
½ cup dry bread crumbs

- Combine the vegetables, soups, salt and pepper in a bowl and mix well. Pour into a greased 9x13-inch baking dish. Top with the bread crumbs.
- Bake, covered with foil, at 375 degrees for 45 minutes.
- May add chopped cooked ham, turkey or chicken if desired.
- Yield: 12 servings.

Approx Per Serving: Cal 96; 33% Calories from Fat; T Fat 4 g; Chol 9 mg; Sod 445 mg; Carbo 13 g; Fiber <1 g; Prot 4 g

Doris Goering, Ames

Side Dishes and Accompaniments • 75

ZUCCHINI ROUNDS

- 1/3 cup baking mix
- 1/4 cup grated Parmesan cheese
- 1/8 teaspoon pepper
- 2 eggs, beaten
- 2 cups shredded zucchini with peel, or 2 medium
- 2 tablespoons margarine

- Combine the baking mix, cheese and pepper in a bowl and mix well. Add the eggs, stirring just until mixed. Fold in the zucchini.
- Melt the margarine in a 10-inch skillet. Spoon 2 tablespoons zucchini mixture for each of 4 rounds. Cook four for 2 to 3 minutes on each side or until brown. Drain on paper towels. Repeat with the remaining zucchini mixture.
- Yield: 6 servings.

Approx Per Serving: Cal 117; 59% Calories from Fat; T Fat 8 g; Chol 74 mg; Sod 226 mg; Carbo 7 g; Fiber 1 g; Prot 5 g

Florine Swanson, Executive Director, Iowa 4-H Foundation

HOMEMADE NOODLES

I have a noodle maker and we make lots of our noodles. My brother and I both like to make them.

- 18 egg yolks
- 2 eggs
- 1 teaspoon vinegar
- 1 cup water
- 3 tablespoons vegetable oil
- 6 cups flour

- Combine the egg yolks, eggs, vinegar, water, vegetable oil and 3 cups of the flour in a bowl and mix well. Add the remaining flour 1 cup at a time, mixing well after each addition until a soft dough forms.
- Roll out a small amount of the dough at a time paper thin and place on a cloth or waxed paper to dry for no longer than 30 minutes. Cut to the desired width and freeze if not using immediately.
- May also process in a noodle maker, using the manufacturer's directions.
- Yield: 6 servings.

Approx Per Serving: Cal 718; 32% Calories from Fat; T Fat 25 g; Chol 707 mg; Sod 45 mg; Carbo 97 g; Fiber 3 g; Prot 23 g

Brooke Lindner, Keokuk

COUNTRY CREPES

1 tablespoon vegetable oil
2 eggs
1 1/2 cups (about) milk
2 tablespoons sugar
1 cup (about) flour
1/8 teaspoon salt

- Combine the oil, eggs, milk, sugar, flour and salt in a bowl and mix well. Adjust the amount of milk or flour if necessary to make a batter that will just coat a spoon.
- Spoon a small amount at a time into a heated and lightly greased crepe pan, tilting the pan to cover the bottom. Bake until golden brown on the bottom, turning and baking until golden brown on the other side. Stack on a heated plate.
- May fill with cheese, bacon or filling of choice. Roll up the crepes to enclose the filling. May top with syrup.
- Yield: 8 servings.

Approx Per Serving: Cal 131; 32% Calories from Fat; T Fat 5 g; Chol 59 mg; Sod 72 mg; Carbo 17 g; Fiber <1 g; Prot 5 g
Nutritional information does not include filling.

Cheryl Ritz, Remsen

CLARA'S PICANTE SAUCE ❖

May be adjusted to mild or hot. Nice and chunky.

5 green bell peppers, chopped
4 quarts red tomatoes, chopped
2/3 cup chopped onion
2 cups cider vinegar
1 3/4 cups sugar
5 teaspoons canning salt
6 jalapeños, chopped
1 teaspoon cinnamon
1 teaspoon nutmeg
2/3 teaspoon crushed red pepper
1 teaspoon mustard

- Combine the bell peppers, tomatoes, onion, vinegar, sugar, salt, jalapeños, cinnamon, nutmeg, red pepper and mustard in a large stockpot. Cook for 2 hours or until of the desired thickness.
- Ladle into hot sterilized jars, leaving 1/2-inch headspace; seal with 2-piece lids.
- Process in boiling water bath for 15 minutes at Iowa altitudes of 1,000 feet or less. Process for 20 minutes for Iowa altitudes over 1,000 feet.
- Serve as a dip for chips.
- Yield: 80 servings.

Approx Per Serving: Cal 28; 4% Calories from Fat; T Fat <1 g; Chol 0 mg; Sod 217 mg; Carbo 7 g; Fiber 1 g; Prot <1 g

Melissa Abbott, Webster City

Side Dishes and Accompaniments • 77

GRANDMA'S SWEET PICKLES

My grandma always makes these pickles. They are enjoyed by everybody.

2 tablespoons salt
2 tablespoons alum
4 cups cider vinegar
1 tablespoon whole cloves
1 tablespoon mustard seeds
1 tablespoon celery seeds
1 tablespoon pickling spice
2 to 3 sticks cinnamon, broken
25 to 30 (or more) small cucumbers
5 cups sugar

- Place the salt, alum, vinegar and spices in a 1-gallon jar, mixing well. Add enough cucumbers to tightly pack the jar. Add enough water to cover the cucumbers. Seal the jar with a tightfitting lid.
- Let stand at room temperature for 4 weeks. Shake the jar once each day to mix the brine.
- Drain and discard the brine after 4 weeks.
- Rinse and slice the pickles. Add the sugar and mix well.
- Store, tightly covered, in the refrigerator.
- Yield: 64 servings.

Nutritional information for this recipe is not available.

Laura Martin, Parnell

ALETHA'S SALSA ❖

24 to 30 tomatoes
16 to 18 green bell peppers, seeded
8 to 12 jalapeños
2 large onions
1 cup cider vinegar
1/2 cup sugar
1/4 cup canning salt
2 to 3 (12-ounce) cans tomato paste

- Dip each tomato into boiling water and remove the skin. Process the tomatoes in a blender until puréed.
- Press green peppers, jalapeños and onions through a grinder.
- Combine the tomatoes, green pepper mxiture, vinegar, sugar, salt and tomato paste in a stockpot and mix well. Simmer for 10 to 20 minutes or until the vegetables are tender.
- Ladle into hot sterilized jars, leaving 1/2-inch headspace; seal with 2-piece lids.
- Process in boiling water bath for 15 minutes at Iowa altitudes of 1,000 feet or less. Process for 20 minutes for Iowa altitudes over 1,000 feet.
- Yield: 112 servings.

Approx Per Serving: Cal 23; 8% Calories from Fat; T Fat <1 g; Chol 0 mg; Sod 440 mg; Carbo 5 g; Fiber 1 g; Prot 1 g

Jodi Thompson, Gladbrook

FUSILLI ALA CAPRESE

Olde Broom Factory Restaurant is on the National List of Historic Places. It serves lunches, brunches, and banquets up to 300.

6 ounces fusilli
¼ cup diced eggplant
¼ cup diced zucchini
¼ cup diced yellow squash
¼ cup julienned red onion
¼ cup julienned roasted pepper
5 tablespoons olive oil
10 ounces marinara sauce
4 ounces mozzarella cheese, diced
Salt and pepper to taste

- Cook the fusilli using the package directions.
- Sauté the eggplant, zucchini, squash, onion and pepper in hot olive oil in a medium sauté pan until very crisp.
- Add the marinara sauce. Simmer for 4 minutes, stirring frequently. Add the fusilli and toss gently for 10 seconds.
- Add the mozzarella cheese, salt and pepper. Toss gently for 5 seconds. Serve hot.
- Yield: 2 servings.

Approx Per Serving: Cal 898; 52% Calories from Fat; T Fat 53 g; Chol 45 mg; Sod 1028 mg; Carbo 84 g; Fiber 6 g; Prot 25 g

Chef John Murtinger, Olde Broom Factory Restaurant, Cedar Falls

RAVISHING RICE DISH

1 (10-ounce) can French onion soup
1 (10-ounce) can beef consommé
2 (4-ounce) cans mushrooms, drained
2 (8-ounce) cans sliced water chestnuts, drained
1 soup can water
½ cup melted margarine
1 (16-ounce) package wild rice
1 cup white rice

- Combine soup, consommé, mushrooms, water chestnuts, water, margarine and rice in a large bowl and mix well. Pour into a greased 9x13-inch baking dish.
- Bake at 350 degrees for 1 hour, stirring every 15 minutes.
- Yield: 10 servings.

Approx Per Serving: Cal 358; 25% Calories from Fat; T Fat 10 g; Chol 0 mg; Sod 622 mg; Carbo 58 g; Fiber 2 g; Prot 11 g

Lisa Schmidt, West Chester

Side Dishes and Accompaniments • 79

RICE AND SOUR CREAM CASSEROLE

6 ounces Monterey Jack or Muenster cheese
1 cup sour cream
1 (4-ounce) can chopped green chiles
Salt and pepper to taste
1½ cups cooked rice
¼ cup shredded Cheddar cheese

- Cut the Monterey Jack cheese into strips. Combine the sour cream, green chiles, salt and pepper in a bowl and mix well.
- Spread a layer of rice in a buttered baking dish. Layer the sour cream mixture, Monterey Jack cheese and remaining rice ½ at a time in the prepared dish, ending with rice.
- Bake at 350 degrees for 30 minutes. Sprinkle with the shredded cheese. Bake for several minutes longer or until the cheese is melted.
- Yield: 4 servings.

Approx Per Serving: Cal 415; 59% Calories from Fat; T Fat 27 g; Chol 70 mg; Sod 629 mg; Carbo 26 g; Fiber 1 g; Prot 16 g

Patti Blum, 4-H Program Assistant, Shelby County Extension

RICE PILAF

1 cup uncooked white rice
½ cup uncooked vermicelli spaghetti, broken into 1-inch pieces
½ cup slivered almonds, chopped
½ cup margarine
2 cups canned French onion soup

- Sauté the rice, vermicelli and almonds in the margarine in a large saucepan. Stir in the soup and mix well. Pour into a greased baking dish.
- Bake, covered, at 350 degrees for 30 to 40 minutes.
- Yield: 4 servings.

Approx Per Serving: Cal 591; 52% Calories from Fat; T Fat 35 g; Chol 4 mg; Sod 1253 mg; Carbo 60 g; Fiber 4 g; Prot 11 g

Joy Corning, Lt. Governor of Iowa, Des Moines

VEGETABLE SIDE DISH

8 slices bacon
1 onion, chopped
1 (28-ounce) can sauerkraut, drained
1 (16-ounce) can chopped tomatoes
1¼ cups packed brown sugar

- Cook the bacon in a skillet until brown and crisp. Remove the bacon to paper towels to drain. Crumble the cooled bacon.
- Add the onion to the bacon drippings in the skillet. Cook until light brown; drain.
- Combine the bacon, onion, sauerkraut, tomatoes and brown sugar in a bowl and mix well. Pour into a greased baking dish.
- Bake at 350 degrees for 1 hour.
- Yield: 6 servings.

Approx Per Serving: Cal 238; 16% Calories from Fat; T Fat 5 g; Chol 7 mg; Sod 1147 mg; Carbo 47 g; Fiber 5 g; Prot 5 g

Wendy Brock, Ames, Extension Youth Development Specialist

VEGETABLE CAPELLINI MASCARPONE

6 ounces capellini
3 artichoke hearts, cut into quarters
1 roasted pepper, julienned
6 slices sun-dried tomatoes
8 slices zucchini
2 tablespoons extra-virgin olive oil
1 tablespoon minced garlic
½ cup vegetable stock
2 tablespoons butter
2 tablespoons grated mascarpone cheese
Salt and pepper to taste

- Cook the capellini using the package directions. Cool slightly.
- Sauté the artichoke hearts, roasted pepper, sun-dried tomatoes and zucchini in the olive oil in a medium sauté pan for 2 minutes. Add the garlic. Sauté for 30 seconds. Add the vegetable stock. Simmer for 3 minutes, stirring occasionally.
- Add the butter, cheese, salt and pepper. Simmer for 2 minutes. Add the capellini. Toss for 15 seconds. Serve hot.
- Yield: 2 servings.

Approx Per Serving: Cal 632; 42% Calories from Fat; T Fat 30 g; Chol 41 mg; Sod 543 mg; Carbo 78 g; Fiber 7 g; Prot 14 g

Chef John Murtinger, Olde Broom Factory Restaurant, Cedar Falls

Holidays and Special Occasions

Wintery Tree

by Rachel Herren
Monticello

Winter snowfall paints a beautiful masterpiece on the Iowa landscape. Rachel Herren, a member of the Scotch Grove Challengers 4-H Club, took this picture near her home in Jones County. This is Rachel's second year in 4-H and the photography project. Rachel is the daughter of Chris and Kelly Herren.

ANISE CANDY ❖

2 cups sugar
2 cups light corn syrup
1 cup water
6 drops of anise oil
Red food coloring

- Combine the sugar, corn syrup and water in a saucepan and stir to mix well. Cook to 280 degrees on a candy thermometer, stirring constantly.
- Remove from the heat and stir in the anise oil and the desired amount of food coloring.
- Pour into a buttered 9x13-inch dish and let stand until cool. Cut or break into pieces.
- Yield: 16 servings.

Approx Per Serving: Cal 212; 0% Calories from Fat; T Fat 0 g; Chol 0 mg; Sod 50 mg; Carbo 56 g; Fiber 0 g; Prot 0 g
Nutritional information does not include anise oil.

Nate Lincoln, Stockton

CARAMELS

This recipe came from my dad's Aunt Phyl Ferguson. We make hundreds each Christmas for gifts.

³/₄ cup margarine
1¹/₂ cups sugar
1 cup light corn syrup
1 (14-ounce) can sweetened condensed milk

- Combine the margarine, sugar and corn syrup in a large saucepan.
- Bring to a boil over medium heat, stirring until the sugar is dissolved. Cook for 10 minutes, stirring occasionally. Reduce the heat to low.
- Stir in the condensed milk. Cook to 240 to 248 degrees on a candy thermometer, hard-ball stage, stirring constantly in a figure-8 pattern with a wooden spoon.
- Pour into a buttered 9-inch-square aluminum pan. Cool until firm.
- Loosen the sides of the aluminum pan and turn out the candy on a cutting board. Cut into squares with a sharp knife. Wrap in squares of waxed paper.
- Yield: 100 servings.

Approx Per Serving: Cal 46; 33% Calories from Fat; T Fat 2 g; Chol 1 mg; Sod 25 mg; Carbo 8 g; Fiber 0 g; Prot <1 g

Chad Harris, Shenandoah

CHOCOLATE-COVERED CHERRIES

2 1/2 cups confectioners' sugar
1/4 cup margarine, softened
1 tablespoon milk
1/2 teaspoon almond extract
2 (8-ounce) jars maraschino cherries with stems, well drained
16 ounces chocolate bark

- Combine the confectioners' sugar, margarine, milk and almond extract in a bowl and mix until smooth.
- Shape into 1-inch balls. Press each ball into a 2-inch circle. Place 1 cherry on each circle and shape to cover completely, leaving the stem exposed.
- Place on waxed-paper-lined trays and cover loosely. Chill for 4 hours or longer.
- Melt the chocolate bark in a double boiler. Dip the cherries by the stems into the chocolate, coating well. Let stand on waxed paper until firm.
- Store in a covered container in the refrigerator for 1 to 2 weeks before serving.
- Yield: 36 servings.

Approx Per Serving: Cal 125; 35% Calories from Fat; T Fat 5 g; Chol <1 mg; Sod 15 mg; Carbo 21 g; Fiber <1 g; Prot <1 g

Barbie Norman, Washington

FIVE-MINUTE MICROWAVE FUDGE

1 (2-pound) package confectioners' sugar
1 cup baking cocoa
1 cup margarine or butter
1/2 cup milk
2 tablespoons vanilla extract

- Combine the confectioners' sugar, baking cocoa, margarine and milk in a microwave-safe bowl. Microwave on High for 4 minutes.
- Stir in the vanilla. Spoon into a 9x13-inch dish lined with waxed paper or foil. Let stand until firm. Cut into squares.
- Yield: 96 servings.

Approx Per Serving: Cal 58; 31% Calories from Fat; T Fat 2 g; Chol <1 mg; Sod 23 mg; Carbo 10 g; Fiber <1 g; Prot <1 g

Cheryl Ritz, Remsen

PEANUT BUTTER MARSHMALLOW FUDGE ❖

2 cups sugar
2/3 cup milk
1 (7-ounce) jar marshmallow creme
1 cup peanut butter
1 teaspoon vanilla extract

- Combine the sugar and milk in a saucepan. Cook over medium heat to 234 to 240 degrees on a candy thermometer, soft-ball stage, stirring frequently. Remove from the heat.
- Stir in the marshmallow creme, peanut butter and vanilla until well mixed. Pour into a buttered 9-inch-square pan. Cool until firm. Cut into squares.
- Yield: 60 servings.

Approx Per Serving: Cal 63; 30% Calories from Fat; T Fat 2 g; Chol <1 mg; Sod 24 mg; Carbo 10 g; Fiber <1 g; Prot 1 g

Rachel Kauffman, Arlington

TRADITIONAL CHRISTMAS FUDGE

2 tablespoons butter
²/₃ cup evaporated milk
1¹/₂ cups sugar
¹/₄ teaspoon salt
2 cups miniature marshmallows
1¹/₂ cups semisweet chocolate chips
1 cup chopped pecans
1 teaspoon vanilla extract

- Combine the butter, evaporated milk, sugar and salt in a saucepan. Bring to a boil over medium heat, stirring constantly.
- Boil for 4 to 5 minutes. Remove from the heat.
- Add the marshmallows, chocolate chips, half the pecans and vanilla and mix well for 1 minute or until the marshmallows and chocolate chips melt.
- Spoon into a foil-lined dish. Sprinkle with the remaining pecans. Chill until firm. Cut into squares.
- Yield: 20 servings.

Approx Per Serving: Cal 195; 42% Calories from Fat; T Fat 10 g; Chol 6 mg; Sod 51 mg; Carbo 29 g; Fiber 1 g; Prot 2 g

Alaina Marie Howe, Weldon

PEANUT BUTTER CUPS

We always prepare this family favorite during the Christmas holidays. We have also made them the past two years at a cookie and candy workshop my mom organizes for my 4-H Club.

²/₃ cup creamy peanut butter
¹/₂ cup confectioners' sugar
2 teaspoons vanilla extract
1 pound almond bark

- Blend the peanut butter, confectioners' sugar and vanilla in a small bowl. Chill for 2 hours or until the mixture is easy to handle.
- Shape by teaspoonfuls into balls and flatten slightly; set aside.
- Place the almond bark in a microwave-safe bowl. Microwave on Medium for 3 to 4 minutes or until melted, stirring after every minute. Spoon ¹/₂ teaspoon of the bark into each of 48 paper-lined miniature muffin cups. Place 1 flattened ball in each cup. Spoon the remaining almond bark over the top, covering completely.
- Chill until firm.
- Yield: 48 servings.

Approx Per Serving: Cal 78; 55% Calories from Fat; T Fat 5 g; Chol 0 mg; Sod 27 mg; Carbo 8 g; Fiber <1 g; Prot 1 g

Kyle Danielle Sexton, Rockwell City

PEANUT CLUSTERS

18 ounces almond bark
2 cups chocolate chips
1 pound salted Spanish peanuts

- Combine the almond bark and chocolate chips in a microwave-safe bowl. Microwave on High for 5 minutes or until melted, stirring after every minute.
- Stir in the peanuts, coating well.
- Drop by spoonfuls onto waxed paper. Let stand until firm.
- Yield: 50 servings.

Approx Per Serving: Cal 142; 59% Calories from Fat; T Fat 10 g; Chol 0 mg; Sod 45 mg; Carbo 12 g; Fiber 1 g; Prot 3 g

Heather Haack, Whiting

TOFFEE

My wife Marjorie's Uncle Gene and Aunt Lucille make this candy Thanksgiving and Christmas holidays to share with family so I wanted to do the same.

2 1/2 cups sugar
2 cups butter
3 tablespoons water
3/4 cup chopped almonds
1 (7-ounce) chocolate candy bar
1/2 cup finely chopped almonds

- Combine the sugar, butter and water in a saucepan. Heat until the butter is melted, stirring frequently.
- Cook to 250 degrees on a candy thermometer. Stir in 3/4 cup almonds. Cook to 300 degrees on a candy thermometer, stirring frequently.
- Pour into a buttered 15x18-inch dish. Cool until set.
- Microwave the candy bar in a microwave-safe bowl until melted. Spread half of the chocolate over the toffee.
- Sprinkle with 1/4 cup of the finely chopped almonds. Chill until the chocolate is firm. Turn the candy out on a flat tray.
- Spread the remaining chocolate over the toffee. Sprinkle with the remaining 1/4 cup almonds. Chill until firm.
- Break into serving pieces. Store in an airtight container.
- Yield: 30 servings.

Approx Per Serving: Cal 239; 62% Calories from Fat; T Fat 17 g; Chol 35 mg; Sod 131 mg; Carbo 22 g; Fiber 1 g; Prot 2 g

Richard D. Johnson, Iowa State Auditor, Des Moines

WASSAIL ❖

4 cinnamon sticks
1 teaspoon whole cloves
½ gallon apple cider
1 quart cranberry juice
1 cup honey
4 cups water

- Tie the cinnamon and cloves in a cheesecloth bag.
- Combine the spice bag with the apple cider, cranberry juice, honey and water in a large saucepan and mix well.
- Simmer for 15 minutes. Discard the spice bag. Serve hot.
- Yield: 18 servings.

Approx Per Serving: Cal 141; 1% Calories from Fat; T Fat <1 g; Chol 0 mg; Sod 5 mg; Carbo 37 g; Fiber <1 g; Prot <1 g

Sean Wehr, Keota

BUTTERSCOTCH ROLLS

2 packages dry yeast
½ cup warm water
2 (4-ounce) packages butterscotch pudding mix
3 cups milk
1 cup margarine
4 eggs
2 teaspoons salt
9 to 10 cups flour
½ cup melted margarine
1⅓ cups packed brown sugar
¼ cup flour
½ cup chopped pecans
1 cup packed brown sugar
½ cup milk
½ cup margarine or butter
4 cups confectioners' sugar
2 teaspoons vanilla extract

- Dissolve the yeast in the warm water in a large bowl.
- Combine the pudding mix, 3 cups milk and 1 cup margarine in a saucepan. Cook, using the package directions; cool. Add the eggs, salt and pudding to the yeast, mixing well. Add enough of the 9 to 10 cups flour to make a soft dough. Knead until smooth on a floured surface and shape into a ball. Place in a greased bowl, turning to grease all of the surface. Let rise until doubled.
- Roll out on a floured surface. Brush with the melted margarine. Sprinkle with a mixture of 1⅓ cups brown sugar, ¼ cup flour and pecans. Cut into rolls and place on 3 greased baking sheets. Let rise until doubled.
- Bake at 350 degrees for 12 to 15 minutes or until light brown.
- Combine 1 cup brown sugar, ½ cup milk and ½ cup margarine in a saucepan. Boil for 1 minute, stirring frequently. Add the confectioners' sugar and vanilla. Beat until thickened. Spread over the rolls.
- Yield: 36 servings.

Approx Per Serving: Cal 377; 31% Calories from Fat; T Fat 13 g; Chol 27 mg; Sod 341 mg; Carbo 60 g; Fiber 1 g; Prot 6 g

Zachary Boswell, Waukee

BIRTHDAY MORNING CINNAMON ROLLS

I am the oldest of six children, and this is the traditional birthday breakfast at our house. We all know how to bake breads, and I have had two state fair entries. The best part of this recipe is that it can be prepared the night before.

4 1/2 to 5 cups flour
1 envelope dry yeast
1 cup milk
1/3 cup margarine or butter
1/3 cup sugar
1/2 teaspoon salt
3 eggs
3/4 cup packed brown sugar
1/4 cup flour
1 tablespoon cinnamon
1/2 cup margarine or butter
1/2 cup raisins
1/2 cup pecans
1 tablespoon cream

- Mix 2 1/4 cups of the flour and yeast in a large bowl.
- Combine the milk, 1/3 cup margarine, 1/3 cup sugar and salt in a small saucepan. Heat to 120 to 130 degrees, stirring constantly.
- Add the milk mixture to the yeast mixture and mix well. Add the eggs and mix until smooth. Stir in as much of the remaining 2 1/4 to 2 3/4 cups flour as needed to form a dough.
- Knead on a lightly floured surface for 3 to 5 minutes or until smooth and elastic. Place in a greased bowl, turning to coat the surface.
- Let rise, covered, in a warm place for 1 hour or until doubled in bulk. Punch the dough down; let rest for 5 minutes.
- Roll the dough into a 12x16-inch rectangle on a floured surface.
- Combine the brown sugar, 1/4 cup flour and cinnamon in a bowl. Cut in 1/2 cup margarine until crumbly. Sprinkle over the dough. Top with the raisins and pecans.
- Roll up the dough to enclose the filling. Cut into 8 slices. Place cut side down in a greased baking pan and cover loosely with greased plastic wrap.
- Chill for 2 to 24 hours. Let stand, uncovered, at room temperature for 30 minutes. Brush with some of the cream.
- Bake at 375 degrees for 25 to 30 minutes or until light brown. Brush with the remaining cream. Invert onto a tray. Drizzle with confectioners' sugar glaze.
- Yield: 8 servings.

Approx Per Serving: Cal 703; 36% Calories from Fat; T Fat 29 g; Chol 86 mg; Sod 406 mg; Carbo 100 g; Fiber 4 g; Prot 13 g
Nutritional information does not include the confectioners' sugar glaze.

Brett Hoben, Wapello

CHRISTMAS T-BRAIDS ❖

We have sold as many as 308 of these for our 4-H Club fund-raiser at Christmas.

8 1/2 to 9 1/2 cups flour
2/3 cup sugar
2 teaspoons salt
2 cups milk
2/3 cup margarine
4 eggs, beaten
2 envelopes quick-rising dry yeast
1/2 cup warm water
1 to 2 tablespoons margarine
1/4 cup flour
3/4 cup packed brown sugar

- Mix 6 to 7 cups of the flour with the sugar and salt in a large mixer bowl and set aside.
- Scald the milk in a saucepan. Stir in 2/3 cup margarine until melted. Let stand until cool. Add the eggs and mix well.
- Dissolve the yeast in the warm water in a small bowl.
- Add the yeast and the milk mixture to the flour mixture and mix well with a dough hook. Add enough of the remaining flour to form an easily-handled dough.
- Knead on a lightly floured board until smooth and elastic. Place in a greased bowl, turning to coat the surface. Let rise until doubled in bulk. Knead again.
- Divide into 4 to 6 equal portions. Roll each portion into a 9x13-inch rectangle on a floured surface. Slash the long sides every 2 inches.
- Combine 1 to 2 tablespoons margarine, 1/4 cup flour and brown sugar in a bowl and mix until crumbly.
- Grease the center of each dough rectangle and sprinkle the filling down the center. Fold the slashed edges over the filling alternately to form a braid, tucking end edges under.
- Place on greased baking sheets. Let rise until doubled in bulk.
- Bake at 350 degrees for 15 to 20 minutes or until golden brown. Frost and decorate as desired.
- Yield: 36 servings.

Approx Per Serving: Cal 205; 24% Calories from Fat; T Fat 5 g; Chol 25 mg; Sod 182 mg; Carbo 34 g; Fiber 1 g; Prot 5 g

Gladbrook Gals & Guys, Gladbrook

Jennie Goodall, Waukee, makes **Play Dough** *by combining 1 cup flour, 1/4 cup salt and 2 tablespoons cream of tartar in a saucepan. Add a mixture of 1 cup water, 2 teaspoons food coloring and 1 tablespoon vegetable oil and mix well. Cook over medium heat for 3 to 5 minutes or until the mixture forms a ball, stirring constantly. Knead on a lightly floured surface until smooth. Store in a tightly sealed container.*

HEART-HEALTHY APPLE COFFEE CAKE ❖

2/3 cup all-purpose flour
1/2 cup whole wheat flour
1 teaspoon baking soda
1 teaspoon cinnamon
1/4 teaspoon salt
1 1/2 cups finely chopped peeled apples
1/4 cup egg substitute
3/4 cup sugar
1/4 cup applesauce
1/4 cup packed brown sugar
1 tablespoon all-purpose flour
1 tablespoon whole wheat flour
1/2 teaspoon cinnamon
1 tablespoon margarine

- Mix 2/3 cup all-purpose flour, 1/2 cup whole wheat flour, baking soda, 1 teaspoon cinnamon and salt in a bowl; set aside.
- Toss the apples with the egg substitute in a large bowl. Add the sugar and applesauce and mix well. Stir in the flour mixture.
- Spoon into a round 9-inch baking pan sprayed with nonstick cooking spray.
- Combine the brown sugar, 1 tablespoon all-purpose flour, 1 tablespoon whole wheat flour and 1/2 teaspoon cinnamon in a small bowl. Cut in the margarine until crumbly. Sprinkle over the batter.
- Bake at 350 degrees for 30 to 35 minutes or until a wooden pick inserted in the center comes out clean. Cool in the pan for 10 minutes. Invert onto a plate. Serve warm.
- Yield: 10 servings.

Approx Per Serving: Cal 167; 11% Calories from Fat; T Fat 2 g; Chol <1 mg; Sod 163 mg; Carbo 36 g; Fiber 2 g; Prot 3 g

Molly Jensen, Hamlin

PINEAPPLE BUNS ❖

Mom and I made up this recipe.

2 yeast cakes
1 teaspoon sugar
1/2 cup lukewarm water
2 (8-ounce) cans crushed pineapple
1/2 cup shortening
1/3 cup sugar
Salt to taste
2 eggs, lightly beaten
7 cups flour

- Dissolve the yeast and 1 teaspoon sugar in the lukewarm water.
- Process the pineapple in a blender until puréed. Pour into a saucepan. Heat to a simmer over medium heat. Stir in the shortening until melted. Stir in 1/3 cup sugar and salt. Cool to lukewarm.
- Add the eggs, mixing well. Add enough flour to make a soft dough. Knead until smooth and elastic on a floured surface. Shape into a ball and place in a greased bowl, turning to grease all of the surface. Let rise, covered, until doubled in bulk.
- Punch the dough down. Divide into small portions and shape into buns. Place on greased baking pans. Let rise, covered, until doubled in bulk.
- Bake at 350 degrees for 20 minutes or until light brown. Baking time will vary according to the size of the buns.
- Yield: 48 servings.

Approx Per Serving: Cal 102; 23% Calories from Fat; T Fat 3 g; Chol 9 mg; Sod 3 mg; Carbo 17 g; Fiber 1 g; Prot 2 g

Barbie Schiefen, Hawarden

Holidays and Special Occasions • 91

ZOETE BROODGES (DUTCH SWEET ROLLS) ❖

My great-grandmother's recipe called for "lard the size of an egg."

2 cups milk
2 tablespoons sugar
1 tablespoon dry yeast
2/3 cup lukewarm (110 degrees) water
3 tablespoons melted shortening
1 teaspoon salt
2 tablespoons sugar
6 cups flour

- Bring the milk just to a simmer in a saucepan. Cool to lukewarm.
- Stir the sugar and yeast into the lukewarm water until dissolved. Let stand until the water bubbles to be sure it is active.
- Combine the milk, yeast, shortening, salt, sugar and flour and mix well. Let rise until doubled in bulk.
- Punch the dough down. Knead for 15 minutes on a floured surface. Let rise until doubled in bulk.
- Roll out on a floured surface. Cut off 1 1/2-ounce portions and shape into rolls. Place on greased baking sheets. Let rise until doubled in bulk.
- Bake at 350 degrees for 20 minutes or until light brown.
- Yield: 36 servings.

Approx Per Serving: Cal 100; 16% Calories from Fat; T Fat 2 g; Chol 2 mg; Sod 66 mg; Carbo 18 g; Fiber 1 g; Prot 3 g

Rebekah Moyer, Rock Rapids

HOLIDAY FRENCH TOAST

8 slices white bread, cubed
16 ounces cream cheese, cubed
12 eggs
1/3 cup maple syrup
2 cups milk

- Layer half the bread cubes, cream cheese and remaining bread cubes in a greased 9x13-inch baking pan.
- Beat the eggs with the maple syrup and milk in a bowl. Pour over the layers.
- Chill, covered with plastic wrap, for 8 hours.
- Bake at 375 degrees for 45 minutes. Serve with syrup or confectioners' sugar.
- Yield: 8 servings.

Approx Per Serving: Cal 458; 59% Calories from Fat; T Fat 30 g; Chol 389 mg; Sod 436 mg; Carbo 29 g; Fiber 1 g; Prot 18 g

Erin Cleveringa, Alton

---

*Kyle Cleveringa, Alton, makes a **Coal Plant** by combining 6 tablespoons each salt, bluing, water and 1 tablespoon ammonia in a bowl and mixing well. Arrange 6 to 8 pieces charcoal or charcoal briquettes in a clear container. Pour the mixture over the charcoal. Drop dots of food coloring over the mixture and watch it grow.*

FAVORITE CASSEROLE

We like to serve this on New Year's Day after the parade. We use leftover potatoes and our own home-canned beans. You can cut the frankfurters into small pieces if you prefer.

- 1 pound frankfurters
- 1/4 cup shortening
- 1/4 cup flour
- 2 cups milk
- 1 tablespoon Worcestershire sauce
- 1 teaspoon (or less) salt
- 2 cups cooked green beans
- 2 cups cooked chopped potatoes
- 1 cup shredded American cheese

- Brown the frankfurters in the heated shortening in a heavy skillet over medium heat or in an electric skillet heated to 360 degrees. Remove the frankfurters.
- Stir the flour into the shortening in the skillet. Cook for several minutes, stirring constantly. Add the milk gradually, continuing to cook and stir until thickened. Stir in the Worcestershire sauce and salt.
- Add the beans, potatoes and half the cheese. Arrange the frankfurters on the top. Simmer, covered, for 15 minutes. Sprinkle with the remaining cheese.
- Yield: 6 servings.

Approx Per Serving: Cal 517; 68% Calories from Fat; T Fat 39 g; Chol 67 mg; Sod 1543 mg; Carbo 24 g; Fiber 2 g; Prot 18 g

Katie Marie Carroll, Avoca

WALKING TACOS

This is a great meal for an outdoor birthday party or youth group gathering.

- 1 pound ground beef
- 1 package taco seasoning mix
- 1 medium head lettuce, shredded
- 1 large tomato, chopped
- 1 small onion, chopped
- 1/4 cup chopped green bell pepper
- 1/2 cup sliced black olives
- 4 ounces Cheddar cheese, shredded
- 1/2 cup taco sauce
- 6 individual packages corn chips

- Prepare the ground beef with the taco seasoning mix using the taco seasoning mix package directions. Place in a serving bowl.
- Place the lettuce, tomato, onion, green pepper, black olives, cheese and taco sauce in individual bowls.
- Give each person an individual package of corn chips in which to combine the ingredients of choice in the package. Mix the ingredients together and enjoy eating from the package.
- Yield: 6 servings.

Approx Per Serving: Cal 773; 54% Calories from Fat; T Fat 48 g; Chol 76 mg; Sod 1463 mg; Carbo 61 g; Fiber 5 g; Prot 29 g

Katie Oswald, Fredericksburg

Holidays and Special Occasions • 93

ALMOND PASTE COOKIES

I received a blue ribbon at our county fair with this recipe from my Dutch grandmother. I always use real butter in it.

1 cup butter, softened
1/2 cup sugar
1/2 cup packed brown sugar
1 egg
2 cups flour
1/2 teaspoon baking powder
2 eggs, beaten
1 cup almond paste
1/3 cup sugar
1 teaspoon sugar

- Cream the butter, 1/2 cup sugar and brown sugar in a mixer bowl until light and fluffy. Beat in 1 egg. Add the flour and baking powder and mix well.
- Reserve 2 teaspoons of the beaten eggs. Combine the remaining eggs with the almond paste and 1/3 cup sugar in a bowl and mix until smooth.
- Layer half the dough, the almond filling and the remaining dough in a greased 9x13-inch baking dish. Brush with the reserved egg and sprinkle with 1 teaspoon sugar.
- Bake at 325 degrees for 45 minutes. Cool on a wire rack. Cut into small squares.
- Yield: 42 servings.

Approx Per Serving: Cal 114; 49% Calories from Fat; T Fat 6 g; Chol 27 mg; Sod 55 mg; Carbo 13 g; Fiber 1 g; Prot 2 g

Sarah Summy, Crescent

CHOCOLATE BALL COOKIES

This has been a Christmas favorite of my father's family since he was a child.

2 cups peanut butter
1/2 cup margarine, softened
1 (1-pound) package confectioners' sugar
3 cups crisp rice cereal
1 (8-ounce) chocolate bar
1 cup chocolate chips
1/4 bar food-grade paraffin, shaved
1/2 teaspoon vanilla extract

- Combine the peanut butter, margarine and confectioners' sugar in a bowl and mix until smooth. Add the cereal and mix well. Shape into small balls.
- Combine the chocolate bar, chocolate chips and paraffin in a double boiler. Cook until melted, stirring to blend evenly. Stir in the vanilla. Maintain at low heat; overheating will cause it to thicken.
- Dip the candy balls into the chocolate mixture, coating well. Place on waxed-paper-lined trays; let stand until firm.
- Yield: 60 servings.

Approx Per Serving: Cal 132; 51% Calories from Fat; T Fat 8 g; Chol 1 mg; Sod 79 mg; Carbo 15 g; Fiber 1 g; Prot 3 g

Erin Dammann, Manning

CHOCOLATE MINT COOKIES

I won a blue ribbon at the county fair with this recipe and the judge liked them so much she asked for the recipe. We always make them at Christmas for gifts.

3/4 cup margarine
2 cups chocolate chips
1 1/2 cups packed brown sugar
2 tablespoons water
2 eggs
2 1/2 cups sifted flour
1 1/4 teaspoons baking soda
1/2 teaspoon salt
2 (6-ounce) packages Andes mint candies, cut into halves

- Melt the margarine in a saucepan. Add the chocolate chips and cook until partially melted, stirring constantly. Remove from the heat and stir until the chips melt completely.
- Combine the chocolate mixture with the brown sugar and water in a large mixer bowl and mix well. Cool slightly.
- Beat in the eggs 1 at a time at high speed. Add the flour, baking soda and salt and mix well at low speed.
- Chill for 1 hour or longer, allowing dough chilled longer to warm slightly. Shape by 1/2 to 1 teaspoonfuls into small balls.
- Place 2 inches apart on cookie sheets lined with foil. Bake at 350 degrees for 10 to 12 minutes.
- Place 1/2 mint on each cookie while warm. Remove the cookies to waxed paper. Let stand for 1 minute. Swirl the melted mint over the top of each cookie. Let stand until cool.
- Yield: 54 servings.

Approx Per Serving: Cal 129; 46% Calories from Fat; T Fat 7 g; Chol 8 mg; Sod 78 mg; Carbo 17 g; Fiber 1 g; Prot 1 g

Jennifer Meyer, Calmar

GINGERBREAD CUTOUT COOKIES

5 cups flour
1 1/2 teaspoons baking soda
1 teaspoon cinnamon
1 teaspoon ground cloves
1 teaspoon ground ginger
1/2 teaspoon salt
1 cup shortening
1 cup sugar
1 egg
1 cup molasses

- Mix the flour, baking soda, cinnamon, cloves, ginger and salt in a large bowl.
- Cream the shortening and sugar in a mixer bowl until light and fluffy. Add the egg and molasses and beat until smooth. Add the flour mixture gradually, beating constantly.
- Chill, covered, for 3 hours.
- Roll 1/8 inch thick on a floured surface. Cut with cookie cutters. Place on a cookie sheet.
- Bake at 375 degrees for 8 minutes. Cool on the cookie sheet for 1 minute. Remove to a wire rack to cool completely.
- Yield: 72 servings.

Approx Per Serving: Cal 81; 33% Calories from Fat; T Fat 3 g; Chol 3 mg; Sod 35 mg; Carbo 13 g; Fiber <1 g; Prot 1 g

Barbie Norman, Washington

Holidays and Special Occasions • 95

MALT BROWNIES

My dad always requests these for his birthday. The recipe is one that my grandmother has used since my mom was a little girl.

1 1/2 cups flour
1 teaspoon baking powder
1/2 cup malted milk powder
1 teaspoon salt
1 cup shortening
2 cups sugar
4 eggs
2 teaspoons vanilla extract
4 ounces premelted chocolate
1 cup pecans

- Sift the flour, baking powder, malted milk powder and salt together and set aside.
- Cream the shortening and sugar in a mixer bowl until light and fluffy. Beat in the eggs and vanilla.
- Add the dry ingredients gradually, mixing until smooth. Mix in the chocolate. Stir in the pecans.
- Spoon into a greased and floured 10x15-inch baking pan. Bake at 350 degrees for 25 minutes or until set.
- Cool on a wire rack. May frost as desired. Cut into squares or bars.
- Yield: 40 servings.

Approx Per Serving: Cal 144; 51% Calories from Fat; T Fat 8 g; Chol 21 mg; Sod 73 mg; Carbo 17 g; Fiber 1 g; Prot 2 g

Holly Workman, Delta

OATMEAL TOFFEE COOKIES

These quick- and easy-to-make cookies are a favorite at 4-H meetings and church youth group. The recipe came from my grandmother.

4 cups uncooked rolled oats
2/3 cup melted margarine
1 cup packed brown sugar
1/2 cup light corn syrup
1 tablespoon vanilla extract
1 teaspoon salt
2/3 cup chunky peanut butter
1 cup semisweet chocolate chips

- Combine the oats and margarine in a bowl and mix well with a spoon.
- Stir in the brown sugar, corn syrup, vanilla and salt.
- Spoon into a 10x15-inch baking pan. Bake at 450 degrees for 10 to 12 minutes or until golden brown. Cool on a wire rack.
- Combine the peanut butter and chocolate chips in a double boiler. Heat over hot water until melted, stirring to mix well.
- Spread over the baked layer. Let stand until cool. Cut into squares.
- Yield: 32 servings.

Approx Per Serving: Cal 167; 45% Calories from Fat; T Fat 9 g; Chol 0 mg; Sod 147 mg; Carbo 21 g; Fiber 2 g; Prot 3 g

Todd Asmus, Webster City

SCANDINAVIAN KRUMKAKE

I won a blue ribbon at the state fair with the holiday favorite from my grandma in Minnesota.

3 eggs
1 cup sugar
½ cup whipping cream, whipped
½ cup melted butter
2 cups flour
½ teaspoon nutmeg
Salt to taste
1 teaspoon vanilla extract

- Beat the eggs in a mixer bowl until light yellow. Add the sugar, whipped cream, butter, flour, nutmeg, salt and vanilla and mix well.
- Bake on a heated krumkake iron until golden brown. Roll immediately on a wooden stick. Remove and let stand until cool.
- Yield: 60 servings.

Approx Per Serving: Cal 52; 44% Calories from Fat; T Fat 3 g; Chol 18 mg; Sod 20 mg; Carbo 7 g; Fiber <1 g; Prot 1 g

Karin Wedeking, Nemaha

SPRITZ

The cookie sheet needs to be at room temperature before pressing the cookies on it for this recipe.

1 cup butter, softened
⅔ cup sugar
3 egg yolks
1 teaspoon vanilla extract or almond extract
2½ cups flour

- Combine the butter, sugar, egg yolks and vanilla in a bowl and mix well. Add the flour and mix to form a smooth dough.
- Divide the dough into 4 equal portions. Place 1 portion at a time in a cookie press. Press into the desired shapes on an ungreased cookie sheet.
- Bake at 400 degrees for 7 to 10 minutes or until set but not brown. Cool on the cookie sheet for several minutes. Remove to a wire rack to cool completely.
- Yield: 72 servings.

Approx Per Serving: Cal 48; 52% Calories from Fat; T Fat 3 g; Chol 16 mg; Sod 27 mg; Carbo 5 g; Fiber <1 g; Prot 1 g

Megan Paulsen, Ringsted

---

*Chelsea Bouchard, Aplington, makes **Cinnamon Ornaments** by combining one 4.12-ounce bottle of ground cinnamon and ¾ to 1 cup applesauce to make a stiff dough. Roll to ¼-inch thickness and cut with cookie cutters. Cut a hole for a ribbon. Dry completely on a wire rack, turning once. Thread with a ribbon and hang.*

UFF-DA QUEEN KRINGLA ❖

This Norwegian recipe from my neighbor won our local Uff-da Day Kringla Contest. My club uses the contest to raise money for our citizenship projects.

1 cup sugar
1/2 cup margarine, softened
1 egg
1 teaspoon baking soda
1 cup buttermilk
3 cups flour
2 1/2 teaspoons baking powder
1/4 teaspoon salt
1 teaspoon vanilla extract

- Combine the sugar, margarine and egg in a bowl and mix until smooth.
- Stir the baking soda into the buttermilk. Mix the flour, baking powder and salt together. Add the buttermilk and flour mixture to the egg mixture and mix well. Mix in the vanilla. May knead if desired.
- Chill, covered, for 8 hours or longer.
- Place the bowl containing the dough in a larger bowl of ice water. Shape by heaping teaspoonfuls into 8-inch ropes on a floured surface. Shape the ropes into figure 8s on ungreased cookie sheets.
- Bake at 450 degrees for 6 to 10 minutes or just until the tops are light brown. Broil for a few seconds to toast the tops. Remove to a wire rack to cool.
- Yield: 48 servings.

Approx Per Serving: Cal 65; 29% Calories from Fat; T Fat 2 g; Chol 5 mg; Sod 75 mg; Carbo 11 g; Fiber <1 g; Prot 1 g

Kendra Larson, Huxley

COFFEE CAN ICE CREAM

Huxley Homemakers have served this treat at Harvest Day at Christensen Forest Preserve for several years.

4 eggs
6 cups milk
2 1/2 cups sugar
1/4 teaspoon salt
4 cups half-and-half
2 tablespoons vanilla extract

- Whisk the eggs, milk, sugar and salt in a saucepan. Cook to 160 degrees over low heat or until the mixture coats a metal spoon. Stir in the half-and-half and vanilla.
- Chill in the refrigerator.
- Place 3/4 cup of the mixture into each of 16 clean 13-ounce coffee cans and replace the lids. Place each can in a larger can and fill the space with crushed ice and rock salt. Place the lid on the larger can.
- Roll the cans back and forth with a partner until the mixture thickens to the desired consistency, adding additional ice and salt if needed.
- May use egg substitute in place of the eggs and omit the cooking step.
- Yield: 32 servings.

Approx Per Serving: Cal 140; 36% Calories from Fat; T Fat 6 g; Chol 44 mg; Sod 59 mg; Carbo 19 g; Fiber 0 g; Prot 3 g

Huxley Homemakers, Huxley

DUTCH ALMOND TORTE

This was a state fair exhibit for me.

¾ cup butter, softened
¾ cup sugar
1½ cups flour
¼ teaspoon baking powder
1 cup almond paste
½ cup sugar
1 egg
2 tablespoons milk
½ cup slivered almonds

- Combine the butter, ¾ cup sugar, flour and baking powder in a bowl and mix until smooth. Press ¼ of the mixture into each of 2 greased 8-inch round baking pans.
- Blend the almond paste, ½ cup sugar and egg in a bowl. Spread half the mixture in each prepared pan.
- Spread the remaining dough over the filling, pressing down slightly. Brush with the milk and sprinkle with the almonds.
- Bake at 325 degrees for 30 minutes or just until golden brown.
- Yield: 16 servings.

Approx Per Serving: Cal 274; 49% Calories from Fat; T Fat 15 g; Chol 37 mg; Sod 100 mg; Carbo 32 g; Fiber 3 g; Prot 4 g

Erin Cleveringa, Alton

CHEESECAKES

This quick and easy family favorite is better if it is prepared the day before it is to be served.

8 ounces cream cheese, softened
8 ounces sour cream
½ cup sugar
1 teaspoon vanilla extract
8 ounces whipped topping
2 graham cracker pie shells
1 (21-ounce) can cherry pie filling or strawberry pie filling

- Combine the cream cheese, sour cream, sugar and vanilla in a blender container and process until smooth.
- Combine with the whipped topping in a bowl and mix gently. Spoon into the pie shells.
- Chill in the refrigerator. Top with the pie filling. Chill for 8 hours or longer. May omit fruit topping if preferred.
- Yield: 16 servings.

Approx Per Serving: Cal 394; 49% Calories from Fat; T Fat 22 g; Chol 22 mg; Sod 304 mg; Carbo 48 g; Fiber 1 g; Prot 4 g

Jessica, Andrea, Lyle and August McIntosh, Dunkerton

Main Dishes

Patterns of Leaves

by Jessica Rohrig
Orient

"Nothing captures the essence of fall better than the changing colors of leaves," said Jessica Rohrig, a member of the Richland Royals 4-H Club in Adair County. She took this picture near Winterset, one of many places in Iowa where people may enjoy the spectacular scenes of autumn. Jessica is an eight-year project member and has received recognition for her work at the Rolling Hills Art Fair. Jessica's parents are Brian and Kathy Rohrig.

LASAGNA D' ITALIA

2 pounds ground beef
2 (15-ounce) cans tomato sauce
1 teaspoon each salt and Italian seasoning
1/4 teaspoon pepper
1 (8-ounce) package lasagna noodles
2 cups shredded mozzarella cheese
16 ounces cottage cheese
1/2 cup grated Parmesan cheese

- Brown the ground beef in a skillet, stirring until crumbly; drain. Add the tomato sauce and seasonings. Cook for 20 minutes, stirring occasionally.
- Cook the noodles using the package directions and drain.
- Layer the noodles, meat sauce, mozzarella cheese and cottage cheese 1/3 at a time in a greased 9x13-inch baking dish. Top with the Parmesan cheese.
- Bake at 350 degrees for 30 minutes. Let stand for 10 minutes before cutting into servings.
- May be cooked in a microwave for 25 minutes.
- Yield: 8 servings.

Approx Per Serving: Cal 544; 45% Calories from Fat; T Fat 27 g; Chol 120 mg; Sod 1421 mg; Carbo 30 g; Fiber 3 g; Prot 45 g

Angela Link, West Point

BAKED SPAGHETTI

1 cup chopped onion
1 cup chopped green bell pepper
1 tablespoon butter
1 (28-ounce) can chopped tomatoes
1 (4-ounce) can mushroom stems and pieces, drained
1 (2-ounce) can sliced black olives, drained
2 teaspoons dried oregano
1 pound ground beef, browned and drained
12 ounces spaghetti, cooked and drained
2 cups shredded Cheddar cheese
1 (10-ounce) can cream of mushroom soup
1/4 cup water
1/4 cup grated Parmesan cheese

- Sauté the onion and green pepper in the butter in a large skillet. Add the undrained tomatoes, mushrooms, olives, oregano and browned ground beef. Simmer, uncovered, for 10 minutes, stirring occasionally.
- Layer the spaghetti, ground beef mixture and Cheddar cheese 1/2 at a time in a greased 9x13-inch baking dish.
- Top with a mixture of the soup and water. Sprinkle with the Parmesan cheese.
- Bake at 350 degrees for 30 to 35 minutes or until bubbly.
- Yield: 12 servings.

Approx Per Serving: Cal 336; 43% Calories from Fat; T Fat 16 g; Chol 52 mg; Sod 572 mg; Carbo 29 g; Fiber 2 g; Prot 19 g

Molly O'Brien, Volga

MEAT LOAF

I chose this recipe because before I made this I had never liked meat loaf.

1½ pounds ground beef
¾ cup rolled oats
¼ cup chopped onion
1½ teaspoons salt
1 egg, beaten
¾ cup milk
¼ teaspoon pepper
⅓ cup catsup
2 tablespoons brown sugar
1 tablespoon prepared mustard

- Combine the ground beef, oats, onion, salt, egg, milk and pepper in a bowl and mix lightly. Place in a greased baking dish.
- Bake at 350 degrees for 45 minutes.
- Mix the catsup, brown sugar and prepared mustard together in a bowl. Spread over the meat loaf. Bake for 15 minutes longer.
- May omit the onion.
- Yield: 6 servings.

Approx Per Serving: Cal 381; 48% Calories from Fat; T Fat 20 g; Chol 133 mg; Sod 821 mg; Carbo 17 g; Fiber 2 g; Prot 32 g

Briana Greiner, Harper

SOUPER MEAT LOAF

I really enjoy this meat loaf recipe, which we found on the soup can.

1 (10-ounce) can cream of onion soup
1½ pounds ground beef
½ cup dry bread crumbs
1 egg, lightly beaten
1 teaspoon salt
¼ cup water
¼ teaspoon soy sauce

- Combine ½ cup of the soup and the next 4 ingredients in a bowl and mix well. Shape into a loaf. Place in a baking dish.
- Bake at 350 degrees for 1¼ hours.
- Blend the remaining soup with the water and soy sauce in a saucepan. Stir in 2 or 3 tablespoons of the meat loaf drippings. Heat to serving temperature. Serve with the meat loaf.
- Yield: 6 servings.

Approx Per Serving: Cal 339; 52% Calories from Fat; T Fat 19 g; Chol 126 mg; Sod 899 mg; Carbo 11 g; Fiber 1 g; Prot 28 g

Derek Winston, Atlantic

Main Dishes • 103

MOSTACCIOLI

This is a recipe that my mom received from some friends when she was a young girl.

1 pound ground beef
1/2 cup chopped onion
1/2 cup chopped green bell pepper
1 (8-ounce) package Italian-style spaghetti sauce mix
2 cups chopped tomatoes
1 (6-ounce) can tomato paste
3/4 cup water
8 ounces mostaccioli noodles, cooked
2 cups shredded mozzarella cheese

- Brown the ground beef in a skillet, stirring until crumbly; drain. Add the onion and green pepper. Cook until tender, stirring occasionally. Add the sauce mix, tomatoes, tomato paste and water. Simmer for 5 minutes. Stir in the noodles.
- Layer the ground beef-noodle mixture and the cheese 1/2 at a time in a greased 2-quart casserole.
- Bake at 350 degrees for 30 minutes.
- Yield: 6 servings.

Approx Per Serving: Cal 562; 32% Calories from Fat; T Fat 20 g; Chol 86 mg; Sod 3617 mg; Carbo 63 g; Fiber 3 g; Prot 33 g

Sarah Droessler, Iowa City

APPLESAUCE MEATBALLS

1 pound ground beef
1 small onion, chopped
1/2 cup applesauce
1/4 teaspoon garlic salt or sage
1 to 1 1/2 cups cracker crumbs
1 (10-ounce) can celery soup
1/3 soup can water

- Combine the ground beef, onion, applesauce, garlic salt and cracker crumbs in a bowl and mix well. Shape into meatballs. Place in a greased 10-inch casserole.
- Mix the soup and water in a bowl. Pour over the meatballs.
- Bake at 350 degrees for 1 hour.
- If sage is used add salt to taste.
- Yield: 6 servings.

Approx Per Serving: Cal 314; 44% Calories from Fat; T Fat 15 g; Chol 62 mg; Sod 784 mg; Carbo 24 g; Fiber 1 g; Prot 20 g

Melissa Abbott, Webster City

CHEESEBURGER CASSEROLE

This is an easy, quick recipe that I've made when Mom is late getting home from work.

1 1/2 pounds ground beef
1/4 cup chopped onion
1 (8-ounce) can tomato sauce
1/4 cup catsup
1/2 teaspoon salt
6 slices Velveeta cheese
1 (10-count) can biscuits

- Brown the ground beef with the onion in a skillet, stirring until the ground beef is crumbly; drain and rinse. Add the tomato sauce, catsup and salt and mix well. Pour into a greased 9-inch-square baking dish.
- Arrange the sliced cheese over the mixture. Top with the biscuits.
- Bake at 400 degrees for 20 to 25 minutes or until the biscuits are brown.
- Yield: 6 servings.

Approx Per Serving: Cal 475; 50% Calories from Fat; T Fat 28 g; Chol 98 mg; Sod 1337 mg; Carbo 28 g; Fiber 1 g; Prot 33 g

Todd James, Prescott

SPICY GROUND BEEF AND BEANS

2 pounds ground beef
1 (15-ounce) can pork and beans
1/4 cup packed brown sugar
1/4 cup barbecue sauce
1 tablespoon molasses
1/4 cup catsup
2 tablespoons Heinz 57 sauce
2 tablespoons mustard
1 teaspoon chopped onion

- Brown the ground beef in a skillet, stirring until crumbly; drain. Stir in the pork and beans. Add the brown sugar, barbecue sauce, molasses, catsup, Heinz 57 sauce, mustard and onion, stirring to mix well.
- Simmer for 10 minutes or longer.
- Yield: 8 servings.

Approx Per Serving: Cal 356; 43% Calories from Fat; T Fat 17 g; Chol 88 mg; Sod 512 mg; Carbo 23 g; Fiber 3 g; Prot 29 g

Leah Franzkowiak, Schaller

Main Dishes • 105

GROUND BEEF PIE

This is a family favorite that is really easy to make.

1 pound ground beef
1 small onion, chopped
1 (10-ounce) can tomato soup
1 (16-ounce) can green beans
5 large potatoes, boiled, mashed
2 tablespoons butter or margarine

- Brown the ground beef with the onion in a skillet, stirring until the ground beef is crumbly; drain. Add the tomato soup and green beans. Bring to a boil. Pour into a greased baking dish.
- Spread the potatoes over the mixture. Dot with the butter.
- Bake at 350 degrees for 15 minutes.
- May be made ahead and reheated or frozen for later use.
- Yield: 6 servings.

Approx Per Serving: Cal 392; 35% Calories from Fat; T Fat 15 g; Chol 67 mg; Sod 719 mg; Carbo 43 g; Fiber 3 g; Prot 21 g

David Oswald, Jr., Fredericksburg

ITALIAN HAMBURGER HELPER

Since salt is a hidden item in many foods, we make homemade hamburger helper to substitute.

1 pound ground beef
½ medium onion, chopped
¼ cup chopped green bell pepper
1 (6-ounce) can tomato paste
1 quart low-salt tomato juice
1 tablespoon onion powder
1 tablespoon garlic powder
½ teaspoon pepper
1 tablespoon Italian seasoning
½ to 1 tablespoon oregano flakes
½ to 1 tablespoon low-salt chili powder
1 to 1½ cups uncooked pasta

- Brown the ground beef in a skillet, stirring until crumbly; drain. Add the onion and green pepper.
- Add a mixture of tomato paste, tomato juice and seasonings, stirring to mix well. Add the pasta. Bring to a boil. Reduce the heat and simmer for 15 to 20 minutes or until the pasta is tender.
- Serve with bread and salad.
- May omit the green bell pepper.
- Yield: 4 servings.

Approx Per Serving: Cal 498; 30% Calories from Fat; T Fat 17 g; Chol 84 mg; Sod 426 mg; Carbo 54 g; Fiber 6 g; Prot 35 g

Bobbi Williams, Greenfield

LAYERED MEXICAN CASSEROLE

This is an easy-to-fix family favorite that my mom adapted from a recipe in a magazine.

1 pound ground beef
1 (16-ounce) can refried beans
1 (8-ounce) jar mild taco sauce
1 (15-ounce) can tomato sauce
6 flour tortillas
1½ cups shredded Cheddar cheese

- Brown the ground beef in a skillet, stirring until crumbly; drain. Add the beans and taco sauce. Bring to a boil, stirring frequently. Reduce heat and simmer, stirring frequently.
- Pour the tomato sauce into a shallow dish. Layer ⅓ of the ground beef mixture and 2 tortillas dipped in the tomato sauce in a greased 8x12-inch microwave-safe dish. Repeat the layers, ending with 2 tortillas. Sprinkle with the cheese.
- Microwave, tightly covered with plastic wrap, on Medium-High for 10 minutes, turning the dish once. Let stand for 5 minutes before serving.
- Yield: 8 servings.

Approx Per Serving: Cal 392; 42% Calories from Fat; T Fat 19 g; Chol 65 mg; Sod 1077 mg; Carbo 33 g; Fiber 6 g; Prot 25 g

Stacie Kienast, Manning

REALLY GOOD RAVIOLI

I am just starting to cook and this is one of the recipes I like to cook.

1 pound ground beef or turkey
1 small onion, chopped
1 teaspoon garlic powder
1 teaspoon onion powder
2 (15-ounce) cans ravioli
1 cup (or less) shredded Mozzarella cheese

- Crumble the ground beef into a 2 quart microwave-safe bowl. Add the onion and seasonings.
- Microwave, covered, on High for 6 minutes or until the ground beef is no longer pink, stirring after 3 minutes; drain. Stir in the ravioli.
- Microwave on High for 5 to 7 minutes or until of serving temperature, stirring after 3 minutes.
- Sprinkle with the cheese. Let stand until the cheese is melted.
- Yield: 6 servings.

Approx Per Serving: Cal 414; 50% Calories from Fat; T Fat 23 g; Chol 162 mg; Sod 984 mg; Carbo 23 g; Fiber 1 g; Prot 29 g

Nicole Williams, Greenfield

Main Dishes • 107

TACO CASSEROLE

My family really likes this and I have found it a quick and easy meal for Fair time.

1 pound ground beef
1 (1-ounce) package taco
 seasoning mix
1 (3-ounce) package corn
 chips
2 cups shredded
 Cheddar cheese
1 medium tomato,
 chopped
1 cup sour cream

- Brown the ground beef in a skillet, stirring until crumbly; drain. Stir in the taco seasoning mix. Add the corn chips and 1 cup of the cheese, mixing lightly. Spoon into a greased 6x10-inch baking dish. Top with the tomato.
- Bake at 350 degrees for 15 minutes. Top with the sour cream. Sprinkle with the remaining cheese. Bake for 5 minutes longer or until the cheese is melted. Serve warm.
- Yield: 4 servings.

Approx Per Serving: Cal 751; 65% Calories from Fat; T Fat 54 g; Chol 169 mg; Sod 1275 mg; Carbo 23 g; Fiber 1 g; Prot 43 g

Valerie Kremin, Manilla

TACO RICE CASSEROLE

My family's favorite, this recipe is easy for younger members of a family to make.

1 pound ground beef
1 small onion, chopped
1 cup uncooked rice
1 (16-ounce) can
 tomatoes
1 (1-ounce) package taco
 seasoning mix
2½ cups water
2 cups shredded
 Cheddar cheese

- Brown the ground beef with the onion in a skillet, stirring until the ground beef is crumbly; drain. Add the rice, tomatoes, taco seasoning mix and water. Simmer for 30 minutes, stirring occasionally. Spoon into a serving dish. Top with the cheese.
- May prepare ahead and bake for 30 minutes at 350 degrees.
- Yield: 6 servings.

Approx Per Serving: Cal 470; 46% Calories from Fat; T Fat 24 g; Chol 96 mg; Sod 864 mg; Carbo 34 g; Fiber 1 g; Prot 30 g

Rachael Taylor, Oskaloosa

TATER TOT CASSEROLE

2 pounds ground beef
2 (16-ounce) cans mixed vegetables
1 (10-ounce) can cream of chicken soup
1 (10-ounce) can cream of celery soup
1 (32-ounce) package Tater Tots

- Brown the ground beef in a skillet, stirring until crumbly; drain.
- Layer the ground beef, undrained vegetables, soups and Tater Tots in a greased 9x13-inch baking dish.
- Bake at 350 degrees for 1 hour.
- Yield: 10 servings.

Approx Per Serving: Cal 482; 47% Calories from Fat; T Fat 26 g; Chol 73 mg; Sod 1398 mg; Carbo 39 g; Fiber 3 g; Prot 26 g

Barbara Voss, Granville

SHEPHERD'S PIE

1 pound beef cubes
Salt and pepper to taste
1 tablespoon butter
4 medium onions
4 medium carrots
1 pound green peas
1 tablespoon butter
2 tablespoons flour
½ teaspoon rosemary
1 cup mashed cooked potatoes

- Season the beef with salt and pepper. Brown the beef in 1 tablespoon butter in a skillet. Add enough boiling water to cover. Simmer until tender, stirring occasionally. Drain and reserve the liquid.
- Cook the onions, carrots and green peas separately in water to cover until tender. Drain each vegetable and reserve the liquid.
- Melt 1 tablespoon butter in a large skillet. Stir in the flour, the beef liquid and the vegetable liquids. Cook until of gravy consistency, stirring constantly. Add the beef, the drained vegetables and rosemary, mixing well. Pour into a deep baking dish. Spread the mashed potatoes over the top.
- Bake at 400 degrees for 30 minutes or until the potatoes are brown.
- Yield: 4 servings.

Approx Per Serving: Cal 417; 28% Calories from Fat; T Fat 13 g; Chol 81 mg; Sod 286 mg; Carbo 45 g; Fiber 11 g; Prot 31 g

Michael L. Fitzgerald, Iowa State Treasurer, West Des Moines

Main Dishes • 109

KOREAN BEEF

This is great served with rice or served cold the next day on salads.

1½ teaspoons sesame seeds
2 tablespoons vegetable oil
¼ cup soy sauce
2 cloves of garlic, minced
⅛ teaspoon salt
1½ teaspoons vinegar
Pepper to taste
1 green onion with top, finely chopped
1 (2-pound) 1- to 2-inch-thick round steak

- Toast the sesame seeds lightly in a hot skillet, stirring constantly. Process in a blender until crushed. Add the oil, soy sauce, garlic, salt, vinegar, pepper and green onion. Process until well mixed.
- Cut the steak into 2-inch-wide strips and place in a shallow dish. Pour the marinade over the steak.
- Marinate, covered, in the refrigerator for 30 minutes or longer.
- Cook on a hot grill for 3 to 5 minutes on each side or until done to taste.
- Yield: 4 servings.

Approx Per Serving: Cal 321; 41% Calories from Fat; T Fat 14 g; Chol 112 mg; Sod 1177 mg; Carbo 2 g; Fiber <1 g; Prot 44 g

Amber Kilberger, Anamosa

FABULOUS FAJITAS

1½ pounds boneless sirloin steak
2 tablespoons vegetable oil
2 tablespoons lemon juice
1 clove of garlic, minced
1½ teaspoons cumin
1 teaspoon chili powder
½ teaspoon crushed red pepper flakes
1 large green bell pepper, julienned
½ cup chopped onion
8 flour tortillas
2 cups shredded Cheddar cheese
1 cup salsa
1 cup sour cream
2 cups shredded lettuce
1 cup chopped tomatoes

- Cut the steak into strips. Brown the steak in hot oil in a skillet.
- Combine the steak, lemon juice, garlic, cumin, chili powder and red pepper flakes in a slow cooker.
- Cook, covered, on High for 2½ to 3 hours or until the beef is tender. Add the green pepper and onion. Cook for 1 hour longer or until the vegetables are tender. Warm the tortillas.
- Arrange the beef mixture, cheese, salsa, sour cream, lettuce and tomatoes in the tortillas, folding to enclose the filling.
- Yield: 8 servings.

Approx Per Serving: Cal 446; 52% Calories from Fat; T Fat 26 g; Chol 87 mg; Sod 537 mg; Carbo 27 g; Fiber 2 g; Prot 27 g

Jody Garrett, Arion

POTATOES AND CREAM

1 (10-ounce) can cream of mushroom soup
4 to 6 thinly sliced medium potatoes
2 to 4 round steaks
1 (10-ounce) can cream of celery soup
Salt, pepper and sage to taste

- Layer 1/2 of the mushroom soup in a greased 9x13-inch baking dish.
- Add 1/3 of the potatoes, the remaining mushroom soup and the remaining potatoes. Arrange the steaks on top. Cover with celery soup. Add the seasonings.
- Bake at 350 degrees for 1 to 1 1/2 hours or until the potatoes are tender.
- May substitute 1 small chicken or 6 ounces tenderized steak for the round steak.
- Yield: 4 servings.

Approx Per Serving: Cal 584; 27% Calories from Fat; T Fat 17 g; Chol 140 mg; Sod 1299 mg; Carbo 50 g; Fiber 3 g; Prot 55 g

Bobbi Rampy, Albia

THE CATTLEMAN

1 cup sliced mushrooms
1/4 cup finely chopped onion
1 teaspoon thyme
1 teaspoon minced garlic
1/2 teaspoon salt
1/4 teaspoon black pepper
2 teaspoons butter
2 cups bread crumbs
1 cup shredded Swiss cheese
4 (6-ounce) thick steaks
1/2 teaspoon minced garlic
1/4 cup butter
1 tablespoon flour
1 tablespoon thyme
1/2 teaspoon salt
1 tablespoon basil leaves
1/2 teaspoon Kitchen Bouquet
1 pint heavy cream

- Sauté the mushrooms, onion, 1 teaspoon thyme, 1 teaspoon garlic, 1/2 teaspoon salt and pepper in 2 teaspoons butter in a skillet. Cool slightly. Stir in the bread crumbs and cheese.
- Cook the steaks to slightly under your desired doneness. Cut a pocket in the side and stuff with the cheese mixture. Place on a baking pan.
- Bake at 350 degrees for 5 to 10 minutes or until done to taste.
- Sauté the remaining garlic in 1/4 cup butter in a skillet. Stir in the flour, blending well. Add 1 tablespoon thyme, 1/2 teaspoon salt, basil, Kitchen Bouquet and cream, mixing well. Simmer over low heat until reduced by 1/4. Serve over the steaks.
- Yield: 4 servings.

Approx Per Serving: Cal 799; 52% Calories from Fat; T Fat 46 g; Chol 195 mg; Sod 1289 mg; Carbo 47 g; Fiber 3 g; Prot 49 g
Nutritional information does not include Kitchen Bouquet.

The Machine Shed, Davenport

Main Dishes • 111

ROAST ON THE GRILL

This is a very easy way to prepare the meat for the grill. Young cooks could do this, and the results are very tasty.

1 (2- to 3-pound) 3-inch-thick boneless beef roast
1 (6-ounce) jar prepared mustard
Salt

- Spread a thick coat of mustard on the top and side of the roast like frosting on a cake. Sprinkle heavily with salt until the color of the mustard does not show through.
- Place coated side of roast down on a hot grill. Cover the top with mustard and salt.
- Grill for 20 to 30 minutes and turn. Grill for 30 to 40 minutes longer or until done to taste. The mustard and salt are pretty much gone after grilling.
- Yield: 10 servings.

Nutritional information for this recipe is not available.

Jon Behrends, Ackley

OODLES-O-NOODLES CHICKEN CASSEROLE

This recipe won first place in Cass County's Best of Iowa Contest.

4 cups uncooked broken egg noodles
2 (5-ounce) cans chicken, cubed
2 cups shredded American or Cheddar cheese
½ cup thinly sliced celery
¼ cup sliced ripe olives
2 packages chicken gravy mix
2 cups boiling water
½ cup milk

- Combine the noodles, undrained chicken, cheese, celery and olives in a bowl and toss lightly to mix. Pour into a greased 9x13-inch baking dish.
- Combine the gravy mix, boiling water and milk in a bowl and mix well. Pour over the noodle mixture, pressing noodles down into the liquid.
- Bake, covered with foil, at 350 degrees for 55 minutes or until the noodles are tender. Serve hot.
- Yield: 6 servings.

Approx Per Serving: Cal 270; 43% Calories from Fat; T Fat 20 g; Chol 135 mg; Sod 1225 mg; Carbo 34 g; Fiber <1 g; Prot 26 g

Louise Knop, Atlantic

CHICKEN STIR-FRY

4 boneless skinless chicken breasts
2 tablespoons vegetable oil
1 bunch broccoli
1 rib celery, finely chopped
1 onion, chopped
1 small green bell pepper, sliced
2 carrots, thinly sliced
8 ounces fresh mushrooms, sliced
1 package stir-fry seasoning mix
$1/2$ teaspoon cayenne
$1^1/2$ cups chicken broth

- Rinse the chicken; pat dry. Cut into narrow strips. Brown in the vegetable oil.
- Add the vegetables. Stir-fry over medium heat for 3 minutes. Add the seasonings and chicken broth. Simmer for 7 minutes or until the chicken is cooked through. Serve over rice.
- May add cornstarch to thicken if desired.
- Yield: 8 servings.

Approx Per Serving: Cal 178; 48% Calories from Fat; T Fat 10 g; Chol 31 mg; Sod 458 mg; Carbo 12 g; Fiber 3 g; Prot 11 g

Brooke Vestal, Emerson

CHICKEN KIEV

I got this recipe from my fourth-grade Favorite Recipe Book. I love to make it and serve it with rice and vegetables.

3 boneless skinless chicken breasts
12 tablespoons margarine
$1/3$ cup flour
3 tablespoons water
2 eggs, beaten
1 cup crushed cornflakes
$1/2$ cup margarine

- Rinse the chicken; pat dry. Cut each chicken breast into halves. Pound the chicken with a meat mallet until thin. Place 2 tablespoons margarine on each half. Fold short ends to the center to enclose the margarine. Fold in the long ends, securing with a wooden pick.
- Roll the chicken in the flour to coat. Dip in a mixture of the water and eggs. Coat with cornflakes. Repeat. Chill, covered, for 10 to 15 minutes.
- Brown the chicken in the remaining $1/2$ cup margarine in a hot skillet, turning frequently. Place in a greased 9x13-inch baking dish.
- Bake at 375 degrees for 20 minutes or until cooked through.
- Yield: 6 servings.

Approx Per Serving: Cal 509; 73% Calories from Fat; T Fat 41 g; Chol 107 mg; Sod 627 mg; Carbo 17 g; Fiber 1 g; Prot 18 g

Gina Coffey, Milford

CHICKEN HOT DISH

This is an original recipe that I cook in my electric skillet.

2 boneless skinless chicken breasts
Vegetable oil for frying
1½ teaspoons Worcestershire sauce
1½ teaspoons soy sauce
2 carrots, sliced
2 large green bell peppers, sliced
2 medium onions, sliced
1 (29-ounce) can chopped tomatoes
1 (16-ounce) package frozen noodles
1 (10-ounce) can tomato soup
Salt and pepper to taste

- Rinse the chicken; pat dry. Cut into strips. Brown in 350-degree oil in an electric skillet, turning to brown all sides. Stir in the Worcestershire sauce and soy sauce. Add the vegetables. Cook until the vegetables are tender-crisp and the chicken is cooked through.
- Cook the noodles using the package directions. Add the noodles and soup to the vegetable mixture. Season to taste. Heat to serving temperature, stirring occasionally.
- May substitute rice for the noodles.
- Yield: 4 servings.

Approx Per Serving: Cal 219; 13% Calories from Fat; T Fat 9 g; Chol 235 mg; Sod 1079 mg; Carbo 110 g; Fiber 6 g; Prot 34 g
Nutritional information does not include oil for frying.

Linda Jensen, Ringsted

CHICKEN ENCHILADAS

6 chicken breasts
2 (10-ounce) cans cream of chicken soup
2 cups sour cream
1 (4-ounce) can chopped green chiles
1 (4-ounce) can chopped black olives
1 (10-count) package flour tortillas
1 cup shredded Cheddar cheese

- Rinse the chicken. Place in a saucepan with enough water to cover. Simmer for 45 minutes or until the chicken is tender; drain. Cut into small pieces, discarding the skin and bones.
- Combine the soup, sour cream, green chiles and olives in a bowl and mix well. Reserve ⅓ of the mixture. Add the chicken to the remaining mixture and mix well.
- Spoon the chicken mixture onto the tortillas. Roll to enclose the mixture. Place in a greased 9x13-inch baking dish. Spread the reserved soup mixture over the top. Sprinkle with the cheese.
- Bake at 350 degrees for 30 minutes.
- Yield: 10 servings.

Approx Per Serving: Cal 416; 49% Calories from Fat; T Fat 23 g; Chol 81 mg; Sod 988 mg; Carbo 28 g; Fiber 2 g; Prot 25 g

Estee Asberry, Exira

CHICKEN A LA MANDY

This recipe was named for my cousin.

1½ pounds boneless skinless chicken breasts
8 ounces fresh mushrooms, sliced
2 (10-ounce) cans cream of chicken soup
1 cup water
1 tablespoon dried onion flakes
¼ teaspoon white pepper

- Rinse the chicken; pat dry. Cut into bite-size pieces. Place in a microwave-safe dish.
- Microwave using the manufacturer's instructions until the chicken is no longer pink. Add the mushrooms.
- Microwave for 1 minute. Mix the soup, water, onion flakes and pepper in a bowl. Pour over the chicken.
- Microwave until 180 degrees on a meat thermometer. Serve over rice or toast.
- Yield: 6 servings.

Approx Per Serving: Cal 245; 33% Calories from Fat; T Fat 9 g; Chol 81 mg; Sod 864 mg; Carbo 10 g; Fiber 1 g; Prot 30 g

Wendy Taylor, Huxley

BAKED CHICKEN BREASTS

8 boneless skinless chicken breast halves
8 slices bacon
8 slices dried beef
1 (10-ounce) can cream of mushroom soup
¼ cup milk
1 cup sour cream

- Rinse the chicken; pat dry. Wrap 1 slice of bacon around each piece of chicken.
- Spread the dried beef in a greased 9x13-inch baking dish. Place the chicken on the dried beef.
- Mix the soup, milk and sour cream in a bowl. Pour over the chicken.
- Bake, covered, at 325 degrees for 2 hours.
- Yield: 8 servings.

Approx Per Serving: Cal 290; 49% Calories from Fat; T Fat 16 g; Chol 95 mg; Sod 638 mg; Carbo 5 g; Fiber <1 g; Prot 32 g

Jacquie Dammann, Manning

---

*Michaela Lauritsen, Exira, makes **Tangy Marinade** by combining 1 cup soy sauce, ½ teaspoon garlic powder and ½ cup each of vinegar, pineapple juice and brown sugar in a saucepan and bringing it to a boil. Cool slightly and use to marinate chicken, turkey or beef in the refrigerator for 6 to 8 hours.*

CHICKEN PITA OLÉ ❖

1 cup chopped cooked
    chicken breast
½ cup finely chopped
    celery
½ cup chunky salsa
⅓ cup fat-free
    mayonnaise
1 teaspoon dried parsley
    flakes
2 pita rounds, cut into
    halves
½ cup shredded lettuce
2 tablespoons fat-free
    Italian dressing

- Combine the chicken, celery, salsa, mayonnaise and parsley in a bowl and mix well.
- Microwave the pita bread, wrapped in paper towels, for 10 seconds. Open gently. Spoon the chicken mixture into the pita halves.
- Combine the lettuce and dressing in a bowl and mix well. Spoon into the pita halves. Serve at once or chill, covered, until serving time.
- Yield: 4 servings.

Approx Per Serving: Cal 169; 9% Calories from Fat; T Fat 2 g; Chol 30 mg; Sod 636 mg; Carbo 24 g; Fiber 1 g; Prot 14 g

Kathy Loupee, Reasnor

GRILLED TURKEY FILLETS

My family likes this recipe so much that my mom planted thyme in her flower garden so we would always have fresh thyme for this recipe.

6 turkey breast fillets
Salt and pepper to taste
Crushed fresh thyme
    leaves to taste
½ cup Italian salad
    dressing
1 tablespoon Dijon
    mustard
1 tablespoon lemon
    juice
½ teaspoon Tabasco
    sauce
6 hot dog buns

- Rinse the turkey and pat dry. Season with salt, pepper and thyme. Arrange in a shallow dish.
- Whisk the salad dressing, Dijon mustard, lemon juice and Tabasco sauce in a bowl. Pour over the fillets, turning to coat.
- Marinate in the refrigerator for 30 minutes.
- Grill over low heat for 10 minutes on each side or until cooked through. Serve on the hot dog buns.
- Yield: 6 servings.

Approx Per Serving: Cal 334; 46% Calories from Fat; T Fat 17 g; Chol 46 mg; Sod 485 mg; Carbo 23 g; Fiber 1 g; Prot 22 g
Nutritional information includes the entire amount of marinade.

Joni Sievers, Storm Lake

MEXICAN FIESTA CASSEROLE

16 ounces ground 90% lean turkey
1/2 cup chopped onion
1/2 cup chopped green bell pepper
1/2 teaspoon dried minced garlic
1 (15-ounce) can chunky tomato sauce
1/2 cup chunky hot or mild salsa
1/4 cup light catsup
2 teaspoons chili seasoning
1 1/3 cups rice, cooked
1 cup frozen whole kernel corn
3/4 cup shredded reduced-fat Cheddar cheese

- Spray an 8x8-inch baking dish with olive-flavor nonstick cooking spray.
- Brown the turkey, onion, green pepper and garlic in a skillet sprayed with olive-flavor nonstick cooking spray, stirring until the turkey is crumbly. Add the tomato sauce, salsa, catsup and chili seasoning. Stir in the rice, corn and 1/4 cup of the cheese.
- Spoon into the prepared baking dish. Sprinkle with the remaining 1/2 cup cheese.
- Bake at 350 degrees for 20 minutes or until the cheese melts.
- Cool on a wire rack for 5 minutes before serving.
- May freeze for future use.
- Yield: 6 servings.

Approx Per Serving: Cal 335; 18% Calories from Fat; T Fat 7 g; Chol 50 mg; Sod 385 mg; Carbo 50 g; Fiber 2 g; Prot 20 g

Kathy Loupee, Reasnor

ORIENTAL LAMB CHOPS ❖

Kevin won a first place in the lamb category and was overall champion teenage winner in the Farm Bureau Iowa State Cook-Off with this recipe in 1994. In 1995, Kevin again was chosen the overall champion teenage winner using a variation of this recipe with pork chops.

6 lamb chops
1/3 cup soy sauce
1/4 cup sugar
1 teaspoon confectioners' sugar
1 teaspoon minced garlic
1/4 teaspoon salt

- Arrange the lamb chops in a single layer in a shallow dish.
- Combine the soy sauce, sugar, confectioners' sugar, garlic and salt in a bowl and mix well. Pour over the lamb, turning to coat.
- Marinate in the refrigerator for 4 to 6 hours, turning occasionally. Drain, reserving the marinade. Heat the marinade to a boil in a saucepan over medium heat.
- Grill the lamb chops over hot coals for 30 minutes or until done to taste, turning and basting with the reserved marinade frequently.
- May substitute pork chops for the lamb chops.
- Yield: 6 servings.

Approx Per Serving: Cal 142; 29% Calories from Fat; T Fat 5 g; Chol 44 mg; Sod 1040 mg; Carbo 10 g; Fiber <1 g; Prot 15 g

Kevin Converse, Fredericksburg

HOMEMADE PIZZA

1 pound ground Italian sausage
2 (7-ounce) packages pizza crust mix
2 cups pizza sauce
1 medium onion, chopped
1 red bell pepper, chopped
1 cup sliced fresh mushrooms
1 or 2 tomatoes, sliced
8 ounces mozzarella cheese, shredded
4 ounces mild Cheddar cheese, shredded

- Brown the sausage in a skillet, stirring until crumbly; drain.
- Prepare the pizza dough using package directions. Fit the dough into a greased 10x14-inch baking sheet; pierce with a fork.
- Bake at 425 degrees for 2 to 3 minutes. Spread with the pizza sauce. Arrange the sausage, onion, red pepper, mushrooms and tomatoes over the sauce. Sprinkle with the mozzarella cheese and Cheddar cheese.
- Bake for 18 to 25 minutes longer or until done to taste. Cut into 2-inch squares.
- Top the pizza with any of your favorite toppings or try using Canadian bacon, jalapeños, ground beef or ground pork.
- Yield: 5 servings.

Approx Per Serving: Cal 691; 43% Calories from Fat; T Fat 34 g; Chol 93 mg; Sod 1678 mg; Carbo 65 g; Fiber 3 g; Prot 34 g

J. C. Christiaansen, Williamsburg

PERSONAL PIZZAS

Margo, who is ten, makes these pizzas with her friends without much assistance.

4 English muffins, split
1 (8-ounce) can tomato sauce
½ teaspoon basil
½ teaspoon oregano
16 slices salami
4 ounces mozzarella cheese, shredded

- Arrange the muffins cut side up on an ungreased baking sheet.
- Combine the tomato sauce, basil and oregano in a bowl and mix well. Spread 1 to 2 tablespoons on each muffin half. Place 2 slices of salami on each half; sprinkle with the cheese.
- Bake at 400 degrees for 15 to 20 minutes or until the cheese melts.
- Cool before serving.
- May substitute pepperoni for the salami. May sprinkle with grated Parmesan cheese.
- Yield: 4 servings.

Approx Per Serving: Cal 394; 48% Calories from Fat; T Fat 21 g; Chol 54 mg; Sod 1616 mg; Carbo 32 g; Fiber 3 g; Prot 20 g

Margo McMahill, Ankeny

PIZZA

Our family has been using this recipe for eighteen years. It is our favorite Saturday night supper. My brother cannot have cheese, so we make a separate pizza for him without the cheese.

1 envelope dry yeast
½ cup lukewarm water
1½ to 1¾ cups flour
1 tablespoon sugar
1 tablespoon butter
1 egg, beaten
½ teaspoon salt
1 (8-ounce) can tomato sauce
½ teaspoon oregano
2 cups shredded mozzarella cheese

- Dissolve the yeast in the lukewarm water and mix well.
- Combine the yeast mixture, just enough flour to make a stiff dough, sugar, butter, egg and salt in a bowl and mix well.
- Knead on a lightly floured surface until smooth. Fit into a greased 15-inch pizza pan. Spread with the tomato sauce; sprinkle with the oregano. Sprinkle with the mozzarella cheese.
- Bake at 350 degrees for 25 minutes or until the cheese melts.
- May top the pizza with any of your favorite pizza toppings.
- Yield: 4 servings.

Approx Per Serving: Cal 436; 35% Calories from Fat; T Fat 17 g; Chol 105 mg; Sod 865 mg; Carbo 51 g; Fiber 3 g; Prot 20 g

Kristel Colvin, Cambridge

PIZZA HOT DISH

This recipe was given to my mom by a neighbor, and has become a favorite for potluck dinners for kids as well as adults.

1½ pounds ground beef
Chopped onion to taste, or 1 teaspoon dried minced onion
8 ounces egg noodles, cooked, drained
3 cups pizza sauce
1 (10-ounce) can Cheddar cheese soup
1½ cups shredded mozzarella cheese

- Brown the ground beef with the onion in a skillet, stirring until the ground beef is crumbly; drain.
- Combine the ground beef mixture, noodles, pizza sauce and soup in a bowl and mix well. Spoon into a greased 9x13-inch baking pan.
- Bake at 350 degrees for 45 minutes; sprinkle with the cheese.
- Bake for 15 minutes longer.
- Yield: 8 servings.

Approx Per Serving: Cal 344; 46% Calories from Fat; T Fat 23 g; Chol 139 mg; Sod 820 mg; Carbo 30 g; Fiber <1 g; Prot 31 g

Adam David Cook, Nemaha

PIZZA QUICHE

This recipe won second place at the Milk Made Magic Sweepstakes at the Iowa State Fair.

3 cups shredded mozzarella cheese
2 cups shredded Cheddar cheese
1 unbaked (9-inch) pie shell
1 (4-ounce) can sliced mushrooms, drained
2 ounces sliced pepperoni, finely chopped
3/4 cup milk
2 eggs
1 teaspoon Italian seasoning
1 (16-ounce) jar spaghetti sauce, heated

- Layer the mozzarella cheese and Cheddar cheese in the pie shell. Top with the mushrooms and pepperoni.
- Combine the milk, eggs and Italian seasoning in a bowl and mix well. Pour over the prepared layers.
- Bake at 400 degrees for 45 minutes or until set.
- Let stand for 15 minutes before serving. Cut into wedges. Drizzle the heated spaghetti sauce over each wedge.
- Yield: 8 servings.

Approx Per Serving: Cal 484; 63% Calories from Fat; T Fat 34 g; Chol 125 mg; Sod 967 mg; Carbo 23 g; Fiber 1 g; Prot 22 g

Erin Summy, Crescent

UPSIDE-DOWN PIZZA

1 1/2 pounds ground beef
1 (32-ounce) jar spaghetti sauce
8 ounces mozzarella cheese, shredded
2 (10-count) cans biscuits

- Brown the ground beef in a skillet, stirring until crumbly; drain. Stir in the spaghetti sauce. Spoon into a 9x13-inch baking pan.
- Bake at 450 degrees for 5 minutes. Sprinkle with the cheese. Arrange the biscuits over the prepared layers.
- Bake for 5 minutes. Flatten the biscuits slightly with a fork.
- Bake for 5 to 10 minutes longer or until golden brown.
- May substitute ground pork for the ground beef.
- Yield: 10 servings.

Approx Per Serving: Cal 538; 47% Calories from Fat; T Fat 30 g; Chol 68 mg; Sod 1421 mg; Carbo 49 g; Fiber 1 g; Prot 27 g

Erin Dammann, Manning

VEGGIE ENCHILADAS

1 (16-ounce) can kidney beans, drained
1 cup chopped onion
2 cloves of garlic, chopped
2 teaspoons vegetable oil
1 cup corn
1 (4-ounce) can mushrooms, drained
1 (16-ounce) jar salsa
8 small tortillas
1 cup shredded Cheddar cheese
2 cups shredded lettuce
2 tomatoes, chopped
½ cup sour cream

- Rinse the beans and drain; mash lightly.
- Sauté the onion and garlic in the oil in a skillet. Stir in the beans, corn and mushrooms. Add ½ cup of the salsa and mix well.
- Spoon ⅓ cup of the bean mixture onto each tortilla; roll to enclose the filling.
- Arrange seam side down in a lightly oiled 6x10-inch baking dish. Spoon the remaining salsa over the filled tortillas.
- Bake, covered loosely, at 350 degrees for 30 minutes. Sprinkle with the cheese.
- Serve the enchiladas with the lettuce, tomatoes and sour cream.
- Yield: 8 servings.

Approx Per Serving: Cal 316; 34% Calories from Fat; T Fat 12 g; Chol 21 mg; Sod 790 mg; Carbo 41 g; Fiber 6 g; Prot 12 g

Ashley Schwaller, Cherokee

HAM BISCUITS WITH CHEESE SAUCE

This is one of my favorite recipes and I am now learning how to prepare it.

2 cups baking mix
⅔ cup (about) milk
2 cups ground ham
3 tablespoons melted margarine
2 teaspoons prepared mustard
1 teaspoon prepared horseradish
3 tablespoons margarine
2 tablespoons flour
½ teaspoon salt
1⅓ cups milk
¾ cup shredded Cheddar cheese

- Mix the baking mix in a bowl with just enough milk to form a stiff dough. Roll the dough into an 8x12-inch rectangle on a lightly floured surface.
- Combine the ham, 3 tablespoons melted margarine, mustard and horseradish in a bowl and mix well. Spread over the dough. Roll loosely to enclose the filling; seal the edge. Cut into 1-inch slices.
- Arrange the slices cut side down in an oiled 9x13-inch baking pan.
- Bake at 400 degrees for 15 to 20 minutes or until light brown.
- Heat 3 tablespoons margarine in a saucepan until melted. Add the flour and salt, stirring until smooth. Stir in the milk. Cook until thickened, stirring constantly. Add the cheese.
- Cook until the cheese melts, stirring constantly. Drizzle over the ham biscuits.
- Yield: 7 servings.

Approx Per Serving: Cal 389; 54% Calories from Fat; T Fat 23 g; Chol 45 mg; Sod 1339 mg; Carbo 26 g; Fiber 1 g; Prot 18 g

Kyle Danielle Sexton, Rockwell City

Main Dishes • 121

HOT HAM AND CHEESE SANDWICHES

Serve with cheese soup in the winter.

1/2 cup margarine, softened
2 teaspoons prepared mustard
1 teaspoon poppy seeds
1/8 teaspoon garlic powder
1/8 teaspoon salt
12 hamburger buns
12 (1/4-inch-thick) slices cooked ham
8 to 10 ounces thinly sliced cheese

- Combine the margarine, mustard, poppy seeds, garlic powder and salt in a bowl and mix well.
- Spread the margarine mixture on the cut sides of the buns. Layer 1 slice of ham and 1 slice of cheese on the bottom half of each bun; top with the remaining bun halves. Wrap each bun in foil. Place on a baking sheet.
- Bake at 400 degrees for 10 to 15 minutes or until heated through.
- Yield: 12 servings.

Approx Per Serving: Cal 321; 49% Calories from Fat; T Fat 17 g; Chol 31 mg; Sod 1030 mg; Carbo 25 g; Fiber 1 g; Prot 16 g

Rachael Thompson, Sac City

MEAT ENCHILADAS

1 1/2 to 2 pounds ground pork
1 small onion, chopped
1 (10-ounce) can cream of chicken soup
1 (10-ounce) can mild enchilada sauce
12 flour tortillas
8 to 12 ounces Cheddar cheese, shredded

- Brown the ground pork with the onion in a skillet, stirring until the ground pork is crumbly; drain.
- Combine the soup and enchilada sauce in a bowl and mix well. Reserve 3/4 to 1 cup of the sauce mixture.
- Microwave the tortillas for several seconds to soften.
- Reserve 4 ounces of the cheese.
- Layer each tortilla with the ground pork mixture, the remaining sauce mixture and the remaining cheese; roll to enclose the filling.
- Arrange seam side down in a 9x13-inch baking pan. Top with the reserved sauce mixture; sprinkle with the reserved cheese.
- Bake at 350 degrees for 20 to 25 minutes or until bubbly.
- Yield: 6 servings.

Approx Per Serving: Cal 904; 56% Calories from Fat; T Fat 56 g; Chol 186 mg; Sod 1227 mg; Carbo 48 g; Fiber 3 g; Prot 52 g

Kacie Menning, Hampton

PORK CHOP AND POTATO SCALLOP

4 (4-ounce) pork chops
1 (10-ounce) can cream of celery soup
½ cup sour cream
¼ cup water
2 tablespoons chopped fresh parsley
4 cups thinly sliced potatoes
Salt and pepper to taste

- Brown the pork chops on both sides in a skillet; drain.
- Combine the soup, sour cream, water and parsley in a bowl and mix well. Alternate layers of the potatoes and soup mixture in a 2-quart baking dish until all the ingredients have been used, sprinkling each layer of potatoes with salt and pepper. Top with the pork chops.
- Bake, covered, at 350 degrees for 1¼ hours or until the pork chops are cooked through.
- Yield: 4 servings.

Approx Per Serving: Cal 392; 39% Calories from Fat; T Fat 17 g; Chol 90 mg; Sod 654 mg; Carbo 33 g; Fiber 2 g; Prot 27 g

Andy Goodall

GLAZED STUFFED CHOPS

This is one of our award-winning recipes, sure to please your family. The stuffing adds a tenderness and flavor which enhances this delicious entrée.

⅓ cup packed brown sugar
¼ cup apple juice
4 (13-ounce) center-cut pork rib chops
3 cups croutons
½ cup apple juice
½ cup chopped celery
⅓ cup raisins
5 ounces apples, peeled, sliced
¼ cup melted margarine

- Bring the brown sugar and ¼ cup apple juice to a boil in a saucepan; reduce heat.
- Simmer for 30 minutes, stirring occasionally.
- Split the pork chops into halves by making 1 cut from the meat side to the bone; leave connected at the bone.
- Combine the croutons, ½ cup apple juice, celery, raisins, apples and margarine in a bowl, tossing to mix.
- Stuff each pork chop with about ¾ cup of the apple mixture. Arrange in a baking pan.
- Bake at 350 degrees for 30 minutes; brush with the brown sugar glaze.
- Bake for 15 minutes longer or until a meat thermometer registers 165 degrees. May cover with foil to prevent overbrowning.
- Yield: 4 servings.

Approx Per Serving: Cal 863; 39% Calories from Fat; T Fat 37 g; Chol 224 mg; Sod 491 mg; Carbo 53 g; Fiber 3 g; Prot 76 g

The Machine Shed, Urbandale

SWEET-AND-SOUR PORK

2 cups water
1 cup rice
1 pound boneless pork, cut into cubes
1 (15-ounce) can pineapple tidbits
1/4 cup packed brown sugar
2 tablespoons cornstarch
1 teaspoon cinnamon

- Bring 2 cups water and rice to a boil in a saucepan; reduce heat.
- Simmer, covered, until the rice is tender.
- Brown the pork in a skillet; drain. Combine the pork and a small amount of water in a saucepan.
- Simmer until the pork is cooked through, stirring occasionally. Stir in the pineapple, brown sugar, cornstarch and cinnamon.
- Cook until thickened, stirring frequently. Spoon over the hot cooked rice.
- May add sliced mushrooms, coarsely chopped apple, mandarin oranges, chopped green bell pepper and/or chopped onion.
- Yield: 4 servings.

Approx Per Serving: Cal 471; 15% Calories from Fat; T Fat 8 g; Chol 69 mg; Sod 63 mg; Carbo 73 g; Fiber 1 g; Prot 26 g

Jerica Rasmussen

FETTUCCINI AND CHEESE PIE

This recipe was given to me by my aunt in Maine, and has become a family favorite.

8 ounces fettuccini
8 ounces bulk sausage, crumbled
1/4 cup chopped onion
1/4 cup chopped green bell pepper
1 cup shredded Colby cheese
1 cup shredded Monterey Jack cheese
2 tablespoons pimento
1 cup milk
3 eggs, beaten
1/4 teaspoon salt
1/8 teaspoon pepper

- Cook the fettuccini using package directions; drain. Rinse with cold water; drain.
- Brown the sausage with the onion and green pepper in a skillet, stirring until the sausage is crumbly; drain.
- Combine the fettuccini, sausage mixture, Colby Cheese, Monterey Jack cheese and pimento in a bowl and mix gently. Spoon into a greased 8x12-inch baking pan.
- Combine the milk, eggs, salt and pepper in a bowl and mix well. Pour over the fettuccini mixture.
- Bake, covered, at 350 degrees for 25 minutes; remove the cover.
- Bake for 15 minutes longer. Let stand for 10 minutes before serving.
- Yield: 6 servings.

Approx Per Serving: Cal 416; 47% Calories from Fat; T Fat 22 g; Chol 161 mg; Sod 587 mg; Carbo 32 g; Fiber 1 g; Prot 22 g

Dawn Taylor, Huxley

EIGHTH STREET LINGUINI

¼ cup vegetable oil
8 ounces grouper, cut into bite-size pieces
8 ounces smoked link sausage, cut into bite-size pieces
8 ounces uncooked salad shrimp
1 tablespoon minced garlic
1 tablespoon Cajun seasoning
¼ cup white wine
10 ounces whipping cream
14 ounces cooked linguini
½ cup grated Parmesan cheese
Chopped fresh parsley to taste

- Heat the oil in a sauté pan until hot. Add the grouper.
- Sauté for 1 minute. Add the sausage and shrimp.
- Sauté for 2 minutes. Stir in the garlic and Cajun seasoning. Deglaze with the white wine.
- Cook until reduced by ½, stirring constantly. Stir in the whipping cream.
- Cook until of the desired consistency, stirring constantly. Stir in the Parmesan cheese.
- Combine the grouper mixture and linguini in a serving bowl, tossing to mix. Sprinkle with parsley.
- Yield: 2 servings.

Approx Per Serving: Cal 1553; 63% Calories from Fat; T Fat 108 g; Chol 470 mg; Sod 3133 mg; Carbo 64 g; Fiber 3 g; Prot 76 g

Jimmy's American Café, West Des Moines

CREAMY TUNA CASSEROLE

5 tablespoons margarine
¼ cup flour
¼ cup chopped onion
2 cups milk
1 teaspoon salt
⅛ teaspoon pepper
2 (3-ounce) cans tuna
1 (10-ounce) can cream of mushroom soup
4 ounces Velveeta cheese, chopped
2 hard-cooked eggs, chopped
3 cups noodles, cooked, drained

- Heat the margarine in a saucepan until melted. Add the flour and onion, stirring until mixed. Stir in the milk, salt and pepper.
- Cook until thickened, stirring constantly. Stir in the tuna, soup, cheese and eggs. Add the noodles and stir gently. Spoon into a baking dish.
- Bake at 400 degrees for 30 to 40 minutes or until bubbly.
- Yield: 6 servings.

Approx Per Serving: Cal 334; 57% Calories from Fat; T Fat 25 g; Chol 133 mg; Sod 1278 mg; Carbo 22 g; Fiber <1 g; Prot 20 g

Jessi Kleitsch, Readlyn

Bars and Cookies

Road Disappearing Into Trees

by Rachel Wadle
Fonda

This photo, which also appears on the back cover, depicts that welcoming country lane, a road that leads a weary traveler home. Home, where the kitchen smells tickle your nose, and the home-cooked meal warms you inside and out. Rachel Wadle took this picture at the Sunken Grove Reserve near her home in Pocahontas County. "It reflects the beauty of Iowa—the peace of nature," she said. A member of the Cedar Leaders 4-H Club, Rachel has been enrolled in the 4-H photography project for seven years. Rachel's parents are Rick and Barb Wadle.

PEANUT BUTTER CHOCOLATE SQUARES

1 cup light corn syrup
1 cup semisweet
  chocolate chips
1/2 cup creamy peanut
  butter
5 cups Triples cereal
1 cup chopped peanuts
1 cup miniature
  marshmallows

- Heat the corn syrup, chocolate chips and peanut butter in a 4-quart saucepan over low heat until smooth, stirring frequently. Remove from heat.
- Stir in the cereal and peanuts. Fold in the marshmallows.
- Press into a buttered 8x8-inch dish with a buttered spoon.
- Chill for 1 hour or until firm. Cut into 1 1/2-inch squares.
- Yield: 25 servings.

Approx Per Serving: Cal 157; 36% Calories from Fat; T Fat 7 g; Chol 0 mg; Sod 80 mg; Carbo 25 g; Fiber 1 g; Prot 3 g

Nicole Voetmann, Ringsted

BROWNIES

1 cup water or strong
  coffee
1 cup butter or
  margarine
1/4 cup baking cocoa
2 cups flour
2 cups sugar
1/2 cup buttermilk
2 eggs
1 teaspoon baking soda
1 teaspoon vanilla
  extract
1 1/2 cups sugar
6 tablespoons milk
6 tablespoons butter or
  margarine
1/2 cup semisweet
  chocolate chips
4 large marshmallows,
  chopped

- Bring the water, 1 cup butter and baking cocoa to a boil in a saucepan. Boil for 3 minutes. Pour over a sifted mixture of the flour and 2 cups sugar in a bowl and mix well.
- Stir in the buttermilk, eggs, baking soda and vanilla. Spoon into an 11x17-inch baking pan.
- Bake at 350 degrees for 25 minutes.
- Bring 1 1/2 cups sugar, milk and 6 tablespoons butter to a boil. Boil for 1 1/2 minutes. Remove from heat.
- Stir in the chocolate chips and marshmallows until blended. Pour over the warm brownies.
- Let stand until set. Cut into bars.
- May substitute a mixture of 1/2 cup butter and 1/2 cup shortening for 1 cup butter.
- Yield: 36 servings.

Approx Per Serving: Cal 185; 39% Calories from Fat; T Fat 8 g; Chol 31 mg; Sod 104 mg; Carbo 27 g; Fiber 1 g; Prot 2 g

Tabetha Anderson, Ringsted
Kristi Guse, Estherville

BLONDE BROWNIES

Our family has always enjoyed this chewy, easy-to-prepare bar.

2 cups packed brown sugar
$2/3$ cup vegetable oil
2 eggs
2 teaspoons vanilla extract
2 cups flour
1 teaspoon baking powder
$1/4$ teaspoon baking soda
1 cup chocolate chips

- Combine the brown sugar and oil in a bowl and mix well. Beat in the eggs and vanilla.
- Stir in a mixture of the flour, baking powder and baking soda. Spoon into a greased 9x13-inch baking pan. Sprinkle with the chocolate chips.
- Bake at 350 degrees for 30 minutes.
- Let stand until cool. Cut into bars.
- Yield: 36 servings.

Approx Per Serving: Cal 126; 40% Calories from Fat; T Fat 6 g; Chol 12 mg; Sod 23 mg; Carbo 18 g; Fiber <1 g; Prot 1 g

Beth Ferneding, Manning

4-H BROWNIES

In 1959, Mrs. Lucille Schuster, my 4-H leader, gave me this recipe to use in a 4-H Demonstration at the Dubuque County Fair. I received a blue ribbon, and have been baking these brownies ever since.

4 ounces unsweetened chocolate
1 cup butter or margarine
4 eggs
$1^{3}/4$ cups sugar
1 cup flour
1 teaspoon vanilla extract
1 cup chopped pecans

- Heat the chocolate and butter in a double boiler until melted, stirring frequently. Let stand until cool.
- Beat the eggs in a mixer bowl until frothy. Add the sugar, flour and vanilla, beating until blended. Add the chocolate mixture and mix well. Stir in the pecans. Pour into a greased and floured 9x13-inch baking pan.
- Bake at 350 degrees for 20 to 25 minutes or until the brownies test done. Cut into bars when cool.
- May spread with your favorite frosting. Dust the baking pan with baking cocoa instead of flour so the bottoms of the brownies are not white. This is especially important if they are to be judged.
- Yield: 36 servings.

Approx Per Serving: Cal 142; 58% Calories from Fat; T Fat 10 g; Chol 37 mg; Sod 60 mg; Carbo 14 g; Fiber 1 g; Prot 2 g

Barbara Lyons, Dubuque

CHOCOLATE CRUNCH BROWNIES

2 cups sugar
1 cup butter, softened
4 eggs
1 cup flour
6 tablespoons baking cocoa
2 teaspoons vanilla extract
1/2 teaspoon salt
1 (7-ounce) jar marshmallow creme
2 cups semisweet chocolate chips
1 cup creamy peanut butter
3 cups crisp rice cereal

- Beat the sugar and butter in a mixer bowl until creamy. Add the eggs, beating until blended. Stir in the flour, baking cocoa, vanilla and salt. Spoon into a greased 9x13-inch baking pan.
- Bake at 350 degrees for 25 minutes or until the brownies test done.
- Let stand until cool. Spread with the marshmallow creme.
- Heat the chocolate chips and peanut butter in a saucepan over low heat until blended, stirring constantly. Remove from heat. Stir in the cereal. Spread over the prepared layers.
- Chill until set. Cut into bars. Store in the refrigerator.
- Yield: 36 servings.

Approx Per Serving: Cal 225; 46% Calories from Fat; T Fat 12 g; Chol 37 mg; Sod 156 mg; Carbo 28 g; Fiber 1 g; Prot 4 g

Kelly Christoffersen, Casey

COCOA BROWNIES

This recipe won a blue ribbon at the Butler County Fair.

1/3 cup shortening
1 cup sugar
1/2 cup semisweet chocolate chips
1/3 cup baking cocoa
2 eggs, beaten
1 teaspoon vanilla extract
1/4 teaspoon salt

- Heat the shortening in a saucepan until melted. Remove from heat.
- Stir in the sugar, chocolate chips, baking cocoa, eggs, vanilla and salt. Spoon into a greased 8x8-inch baking pan.
- Bake at 350 degrees for 25 to 30 minutes or until the brownies test done.
- Yield: 9 servings.

Approx Per Serving: Cal 222; 45% Calories from Fat; T Fat 12 g; Chol 47 mg; Sod 75 mg; Carbo 30 g; Fiber 2 g; Prot 2 g

Chelsea Bouchard, Aplington

GRANDMA A'S BROWNIES

1 cup margarine
1/4 cup baking cocoa
2 cups sugar
4 eggs
1 teaspoon vanilla extract
1/8 teaspoon salt
1 3/4 cups flour

- Heat the margarine and baking cocoa in a saucepan over low heat until smooth, stirring frequently.
- Beat the sugar and eggs in a mixer bowl until blended. Stir in the vanilla and salt. Add the margarine mixture and flour alternately, beating well after each addition. Spoon into a greased 11x17-inch baking pan.
- Bake at 350 degrees for 20 minutes; do not overbake.
- Cut into bars while warm. May frost with confectioners' sugar frosting.
- Yield: 36 servings.

Approx Per Serving: Cal 120; 42% Calories from Fat; T Fat 6 g; Chol 24 mg; Sod 74 mg; Carbo 16 g; Fiber <1 g; Prot 2 g

Alicia, Briana and Lindsey Black, Ringsted

THE GREAT AMERICAN BROWNIE

1 cup sugar
1/2 cup melted butter or margarine
2 eggs
1 teaspoon vanilla extract
1/2 cup flour
1/3 cup baking cocoa
1/4 teaspoon baking powder
1/4 teaspoon salt

- Combine the sugar and butter in a bowl and mix well. Stir in the eggs and vanilla. Add the flour, baking cocoa, baking powder and salt and mix well. Spoon into a greased 9x9-inch baking pan.
- Bake at 350 degrees for 20 to 25 minutes or until the brownies test done. Let stand until cool. Cut into bars.
- May spread with your favorite frosting. May add 1/2 cup chopped nuts.
- Yield: 24 servings.

Approx Per Serving: Cal 85; 45% Calories from Fat; T Fat 4 g; Chol 28 mg; Sod 70 mg; Carbo 11 g; Fiber <1 g; Prot 1 g

Jared Fabi, West Des Moines

Bars • 131

EASY BROWNIES

Fast, easy and delicious!

2 cups sugar
1½ cups flour
1 cup shortening
⅔ cup baking cocoa
2 teaspoons vanilla extract
1 teaspoon salt
4 eggs
½ cup chopped pecans
¼ cup confectioners' sugar

- Combine the sugar, flour, shortening, baking cocoa, vanilla, salt and eggs in a mixer bowl.
- Beat for 3 minutes or until blended, scraping the bowl occasionally. Stir in the pecans. Spoon into a 9x13-inch baking pan.
- Bake at 350 degrees for 25 to 30 minutes or until the brownies test done.
- Let stand until cool. Sprinkle with the confectioners' sugar. Cut into bars.
- Yield: 36 servings.

Approx Per Serving: Cal 138; 48% Calories from Fat; T Fat 8 g; Chol 24 mg; Sod 67 mg; Carbo 17 g; Fiber 1 g; Prot 2 g

Kara Rechterman, Tipton

MINT BROWNIES

1 (16-ounce) can chocolate syrup
1 cup sugar
1 cup flour
½ cup melted margarine
4 eggs
1 teaspoon vanilla extract
1 (1-pound) package confectioners' sugar
5⅓ tablespoons margarine, softened
¼ cup milk
15 drops of peppermint extract
Green food coloring
2 cups semisweet chocolate chips
½ cup margarine

- Combine the chocolate syrup, sugar, flour, ½ cup melted margarine, eggs and vanilla in a bowl and mix well. Spoon into a greased and floured 9x13-inch baking pan.
- Bake at 350 degrees for 15 to 20 minutes. Let stand until cool.
- Beat the confectioners' sugar, 5⅓ tablespoons margarine, milk and flavoring in a mixer bowl until of spreading consistency, scraping the bowl occasionally. Beat in the desired amount of green food coloring. Spread over the prepared layer.
- Let stand until set.
- Heat the chocolate chips and ½ cup margarine in a double boiler until smooth, stirring frequently. Spread over the prepared layers.
- Let stand until set. Cut into 3x4-inch bars.
- Yield: 12 servings.

Approx Per Serving: Cal 676; 39% Calories from Fat; T Fat 31 g; Chol 71 mg; Sod 302 mg; Carbo 103 g; Fiber 3 g; Prot 5 g

Larra Souer, Wapello

CARAMEL CHOCOLATE SQUARES

1 (14-ounce) package light caramels
$1/3$ cup evaporated milk
1 (2-layer) package German chocolate cake mix
$3/4$ cup butter or margarine, softened
$1/3$ cup evaporated milk
1 cup chopped walnuts
1 cup semisweet chocolate chips

- Heat the caramels and $1/3$ cup evaporated milk in a saucepan until smooth, stirring frequently.
- Combine the cake mix, butter, $1/3$ cup evaporated milk and walnuts in a bowl, stirring until the mixture forms a ball. Press $1/2$ of the mixture into a greased and floured 9x13-inch baking pan.
- Bake at 325 degrees for 6 minutes. Sprinkle with the chocolate chips. Drizzle with the caramel mixture. Crumble the remaining cake mixture over the top.
- Bake for 15 to 18 minutes longer. Cool slightly.
- Chill for 30 minutes or until set. Cut into 2-inch squares.
- Yield: 24 servings.

Approx Per Serving: Cal 279; 46% Calories from Fat; T Fat 15 g; Chol 19 mg; Sod 307 mg; Carbo 36 g; Fiber 1 g; Prot 3 g

Jessica Schechtman, Earlville

CHIPPER BARS

2 cups quick-cooking oats
1 cup flour
1 cup packed brown sugar
$3/4$ cup butter or margarine, softened
$1/2$ teaspoon baking soda
$1/2$ teaspoon salt
1 (14-ounce) can sweetened condensed milk
$1/3$ cup peanut butter
1 cup semisweet chocolate chips

- Combine the oats, flour, brown sugar, butter, baking soda and salt in a bowl, stirring until crumbly. Reserve $1 1/2$ cups of the crumb mixture. Press the remaining mixture over the bottom of a greased 9x13-inch baking pan.
- Combine the condensed milk and peanut butter in a bowl and mix well. Pour over the prepared layer. Sprinkle with the chocolate chips. Pat the reserved crumb mixture over the chocolate chips.
- Bake at 350 degrees for 25 to 30 minutes or until brown.
- Let stand until cool. Cut into bars.
- Yield: 36 servings.

Approx Per Serving: Cal 155; 43% Calories from Fat; T Fat 8 g; Chol 14 mg; Sod 108 mg; Carbo 20 g; Fiber 1 g; Prot 3 g

Laurie Hrdlicka, Lawler

FROSTED CRISPY BARS

My Grandma Foster makes these bars as a special treat for me!

2 cups sugar
2 cups light corn syrup
3 cups peanut butter
1 (13-ounce) package crisp rice cereal
2 cups semisweet chocolate chips
1 cup butterscotch chips

- Combine the sugar and corn syrup in a saucepan. Heat until the sugar dissolves, stirring constantly. Stir in the peanut butter. Pour over the cereal, stirring to coat. Press into a 9x13-inch dish.
- Heat the chocolate chips and butterscotch chips in a double boiler until smooth, stirring frequently. Spread over the prepared layer.
- Let stand until set. Cut into bars.
- Yield: 36 servings.

Approx Per Serving: Cal 330; 38% Calories from Fat; T Fat 15 g; Chol <1 mg; Sod 252 mg; Carbo 48 g; Fiber 2 g; Prot 6 g

Alex Foster, Clive

MARBLE FUDGE BARS

This recipe was handed down from my great-grandmother, Laura Muller.

8 ounces cream cheese, softened
1/3 cup sugar
1 egg
3/4 cup water
1/2 cup margarine
1 1/2 ounces semisweet chocolate
2 cups flour
2 cups sugar
1/2 cup sour cream
2 eggs
1 teaspoon baking soda
1/2 teaspoon salt
1 cup semisweet chocolate chips

- Beat the cream cheese, 1/3 cup sugar and 1 egg in a mixer bowl until smooth.
- Bring the water, margarine and semisweet chocolate to a boil in a saucepan. Boil until blended, stirring frequently. Remove from heat. Stir in a mixture of the flour and 2 cups sugar. Add the sour cream, 2 eggs, baking soda and salt and mix well. Spoon into a greased and floured 11x17-inch baking pan.
- Drop the cream cheese mixture by spoonfuls over the prepared layer. Cut gently through the layers with a knife to marbleize. Sprinkle with the chocolate chips.
- Bake at 375 degrees for 30 minutes. Cut into bars when cool.
- Yield: 24 servings.

Approx Per Serving: Cal 242; 41% Calories from Fat; T Fat 12 g; Chol 39 mg; Sod 163 mg; Carbo 34 g; Fiber 1 g; Prot 3 g

Renee Horner, Ackley

MILLION DOLLAR BARS

The original recipe was for Butterscotch Krinkles, but my mom called them Million Dollar Bars because they were so expensive to make!

1 cup creamy peanut butter
1 cup butterscotch chips
8 cups crisp rice cereal
2 cups milk chocolate chips
½ cup sugar
¼ cup margarine
¼ cup water

- Combine the peanut butter and butterscotch chips in a microwave-safe dish.
- Microwave until blended, stirring frequently. Stir in the cereal. Pat ½ to ⅔ of the cereal mixture in a buttered 11x17-inch dish.
- Freeze while preparing the remaining part of the recipe.
- Combine the chocolate chips, sugar, margarine and water in a microwave-safe dish.
- Microwave until blended, stirring frequently. Spread over the prepared layer. Pat the remaining cereal mixture over the top.
- Freeze until set. Cut into bars. Serve frozen or chilled.
- Yield: 36 servings.

Approx Per Serving: Cal 161; 49% Calories from Fat; T Fat 9 g; Chol 2 mg; Sod 136 mg; Carbo 18 g; Fiber 1 g; Prot 3 g

Kathy Kuhlmann Paul, Swea City

TAKE-ALONG BREAKFAST BARS

For a quick and convenient breakfast on the go.

¾ cup rolled oats
¾ cup all-purpose flour
⅓ cup packed brown sugar
¼ cup whole wheat flour
2 teaspoons baking powder
1 cup milk
½ cup peanut butter
¼ cup vegetable oil
½ teaspoon vanilla extract
2 eggs
½ cup strawberry jam

- Combine the oats, all-purpose flour, brown sugar, whole wheat flour and baking powder in a bowl and mix well.
- Combine the milk, peanut butter, oil, vanilla and eggs in a bowl, whisking until blended. Add the oat mixture, stirring until moistened. Spread into an 8x8-inch baking pan sprayed with nonstick cooking spray.
- Drop the jam by tablespoons over the prepared layer. Swirl the jam through the prepared layer with a knife.
- Bake at 350 degrees for 35 to 40 minutes.
- Cool in the pan on a wire rack. Cut into bars.
- May substitute your favorite jam for the strawberry jam.
- Yield: 16 servings.

Approx Per Serving: Cal 180; 43% Calories from Fat; T Fat 9 g; Chol 29 mg; Sod 98 mg; Carbo 22 g; Fiber 1 g; Prot 5 g

Shelby Kent, Algona

HO! HO! BARS

Great to serve at 4-H meetings.

1 (2-layer) package chocolate cake mix
1½ cups milk
5 tablespoons flour
1 cup sugar
1 cup shortening
½ cup margarine
1 teaspoon vanilla extract
1 cup sugar
1 cup packed brown sugar
½ cup milk
½ cup margarine
1 cup semisweet chocolate chips
1 teaspoon vanilla extract

- Prepare the cake using package directions. Spoon into two 9x13-inch cake pans.
- Bake using package directions for 15 minutes. Let stand until cool.
- Combine 1½ cups milk and flour in a saucepan. Cook until thickened, stirring constantly. Cool.
- Beat 1 cup sugar, shortening, ½ cup margarine and 1 teaspoon vanilla in a mixer bowl until creamy. Stir in the milk mixture.
- Beat for 8 minutes, scraping the bowl occasionally. Spread over the baked layers.
- Chill for 1 hour.
- Bring 1 cup sugar, brown sugar, ½ cup milk and ½ cup margarine to a boil.
- Boil for 2 minutes, stirring occasionally. Remove from heat. Stir in the chocolate chips and 1 teaspoon vanilla.
- Beat until cool. Pour over the prepared layers. Cut into bars.
- May freeze for future use.
- Yield: 48 servings.

Approx Per Serving: Cal 190; 51% Calories from Fat; T Fat 11 g; Chol 1 mg; Sod 139 mg; Carbo 23 g; Fiber <1 g; Prot 1 g

Tom Carroll, Avoca

QUICK AND EASY PEANUT BUTTER COOKIES

This is a favorite after-school snack at my house. It is easy to prepare and fun to eat, especially if you like peanut butter.

½ cup sugar
½ cup corn syrup
¾ cup peanut butter
1 teaspoon vanilla extract
2 cups Special-K

- Bring the sugar and corn syrup to a boil in a saucepan. Remove from heat. Stir in the peanut butter and vanilla.
- Pour the peanut butter mixture over the cereal in a bowl, stirring to coat. Drop by spoonfuls onto a waxed-paper-lined cookie sheet.
- Let stand until set.
- Yield: 20 servings.

Approx Per Serving: Cal 110; 37% Calories from Fat; T Fat 5 g; Chol <1 mg; Sod 82 mg; Carbo 15 g; Fiber 1 g; Prot 3 g

Shelli Smith, Columbus Junction

CHOCOLATE CHIP COOKIES

2½ cups shortening
2 cups packed brown sugar
2 cups sugar
5 eggs
5 teaspoons vanilla extract
6½ cups flour
2½ teaspoons baking powder
1 teaspoon salt
2 cups miniature chocolate chips

- Beat the shortening, brown sugar and sugar in a mixer bowl until creamy. Add the eggs and vanilla.
- Beat until light and fluffy. Add the flour, baking powder and salt.
- Beat until blended. Stir in the chocolate chips. Drop the dough with a cookie scoop onto an ungreased cookie sheet.
- Bake at 325 degrees for 15 minutes or until light brown.
- Cool on cookie sheet for 2 minutes. Remove to a wire rack to cool completely.
- May substitute a mixture of 1 cup butter and 1½ cups shortening for the shortening.
- Yield: 72 servings.

Approx Per Serving: Cal 186; 45% Calories from Fat; T Fat 9 g; Chol 15 mg; Sod 48 mg; Carbo 24 g; Fiber 1 g; Prot 2 g

Alex Deutmeyer, New Vienna

CHOCOLATE CHIP PUDDING COOKIES

My grandmother sent me this recipe, and it has been my favorite ever since.

2 cups flour
1 cup margarine, softened
¾ cup packed brown sugar
¼ cup sugar
1 (4-ounce) package vanilla pudding and pie filling mix
2 eggs
1 teaspoon baking soda
1 teaspoon vanilla extract
½ teaspoon salt
1 cup semisweet chocolate chips
½ cup rolled oats

- Combine the flour, margarine, brown sugar, sugar, pudding mix, eggs, baking soda, vanilla and salt in a mixer bowl.
- Beat until blended, scraping the bowl occasionally. Stir in the chocolate chips and oats. Drop by spoonfuls onto an ungreased cookie sheet.
- Bake at 350 degrees for 7 to 10 minutes or until light brown. Cool on cookie sheet for 2 minutes. Remove to a wire rack to cool completely.
- May substitute vanilla instant pudding mix for the vanilla pudding and pie filling mix.
- Yield: 24 servings.

Approx Per Serving: Cal 195; 46% Calories from Fat; T Fat 10 g; Chol 18 mg; Sod 204 mg; Carbo 25 g; Fiber 1 g; Prot 2 g

Emily Northey, Spirit Lake

GOLD RIBBON CHOCOLATE CHIP COOKIES

I entered these cookies, my first year in 4-H, in the open class at the Polk County Fair. They won a gold ribbon for Best of Class.

2 cups sugar
1½ cups margarine, softened
1 cup packed brown sugar
4 eggs
2 teaspoons vanilla extract
1 teaspoon butter flavoring
1 teaspoon black walnut extract
4½ cups flour
2 teaspoons baking soda
2 teaspoons salt
2 cups semisweet chocolate chips

- Beat the sugar, margarine, brown sugar, eggs and flavorings in a mixer bowl until creamy, scraping the bowl occasionally.
- Add the flour, baking soda and salt and mix well. Stir in the chocolate chips. Drop by spoonfuls onto a cookie sheet.
- Bake at 350 degrees for 10 minutes.
- Cool on cookie sheet for 2 minutes. Remove to a wire rack to cool completely.
- Yield: 54 servings.

Approx Per Serving: Cal 161; 39% Calories from Fat; T Fat 7 g; Chol 16 mg; Sod 176 mg; Carbo 23 g; Fiber 1 g; Prot 2 g

Melissa Remhof, Urbandale

SCRUMPTIOUS CHOCOLATE CHIP COOKIES

⅔ cup plus 3½ tablespoons butter-flavor shortening
½ cup butter, softened
1 cup sugar
1 cup packed brown sugar
2 eggs
2 teaspoons vanilla extract
3¼ cups sifted flour
1 teaspoon baking soda
1 teaspoon salt
2 cups semisweet chocolate chips

- Beat the shortening, butter, sugar, brown sugar, eggs and vanilla in a mixer bowl until creamy, scraping the bowl occasionally. Add the flour, baking soda and salt and mix well. Stir in the chocolate chips. Drop by spoonfuls onto a cookie sheet.
- Bake at 375 degrees for 10 to 12 minutes or until light brown.
- Cool on cookie sheet for 2 minutes. Remove to a wire rack to cool completely.
- May substitute "M & M's" Chocolate Candies for the chocolate chips.
- Yield: 36 servings.

Approx Per Serving: Cal 195; 48% Calories from Fat; T Fat 11 g; Chol 19 mg; Sod 115 mg; Carbo 25 g; Fiber 1 g; Prot 2 g

Amanda Knuth, Cascade

BLACK BEAR MOLASSES FOREST COOKIES

These cookies have a cake consistency, but not too sweet. They are "beary" good!

3 cups all-purpose flour
1 cup whole wheat flour
1 1/2 teaspoons cinnamon
1 teaspoon nutmeg
1 teaspoon baking soda
1/2 teaspoon ground cloves
1/2 teaspoon salt
1 cup butter, softened
1/2 cup packed brown sugar
1/2 cup sugar
1 egg, beaten
1/2 cup molasses
1 teaspoon vanilla extract

- Sift the all-purpose flour, whole wheat flour, cinnamon, nutmeg, baking soda, cloves and salt together.
- Beat the butter, brown sugar and sugar in a mixer bowl until creamy. Add the egg, molasses and vanilla.
- Beat until light and fluffy. Add the dry ingredients gradually, beating constantly until mixed. Shape into a ball; wrap with plastic wrap.
- Chill for 1 hour. Roll 1/8 to 1/4 inch thick on a lightly floured surface. Cut with a cookie cutter dipped in flour. Arrange the cookies on an ungreased cookie sheet.
- Bake at 350 degrees for 8 to 10 minutes or just until firm.
- Cool on cookie sheet for 2 minutes. Remove to a wire rack to cool completely. Decorate as desired.
- Yield: 72 servings.

Approx Per Serving: Cal 64; 37% Calories from Fat; T Fat 3 g; Chol 10 mg; Sod 55 mg; Carbo 9 g; Fiber <1 g; Prot 1 g

Tristan Workman, Delta

CHOCOLATE CRUNCHES

1 cup butter, softened
1/2 cup sugar
3 tablespoons milk
1 egg yolk
1 teaspoon vanilla extract
2 1/2 cups sifted flour
1/8 teaspoon salt
3/4 cup crushed cornflakes
1 cup semisweet chocolate chips

- Beat the butter in a mixer bowl until creamy. Add the sugar gradually, beating constantly until light and fluffy. Add the milk, egg yolk and vanilla and mix well.
- Add a sifted mixture of the flour and salt, beating until smooth. Stir in the cornflakes and chocolate chips. Drop by teaspoonfuls onto an ungreased cookie sheet.
- Bake at 375 degrees for 15 minutes or until light brown.
- Cool on cookie sheet for 2 minutes. Remove to a wire rack to cool completely.
- Yield: 60 servings.

Approx Per Serving: Cal 70; 51% Calories from Fat; T Fat 4 g; Chol 12 mg; Sod 46 mg; Carbo 8 g; Fiber <1 g; Prot 1 g

Rosalind Kirsch, Wesley

Cookies • 139

CHOCOLATE PEANUT BUTTER COOKIES

2 cups sugar
1 1/4 cups margarine, softened
2 eggs
2 teaspoons vanilla extract
2 cups flour
3/4 cup baking cocoa
1 teaspoon baking soda
1/2 teaspoon salt
1/2 to 3/4 cup peanut butter chips

- Beat the sugar and margarine in a mixer bowl until creamy. Add the eggs and vanilla.
- Beat until light and fluffy. Stir in a sifted mixture of the flour, baking cocoa, baking soda and salt. Fold in the peanut butter chips. Drop by teaspoonfuls onto a cookie sheet.
- Bake at 350 degrees for 10 to 12 minutes or until firm. Cool on cookie sheet for 2 minutes. Remove to a wire rack to cool completely.
- May spread the dough in a 10x17-inch baking pan. Bake at 350 degrees for 25 to 30 minutes or until a wooden pick inserted in center comes out clean. Cut into bars when cool.
- Yield: 36 servings.

Approx Per Serving: Cal 151; 46% Calories from Fat; T Fat 8 g; Chol 12 mg; Sod 140 mg; Carbo 19 g; Fiber 1 g; Prot 2 g

Travis James, Prescott

GRANDPA'S OATMEAL-RAISIN COOKIES

My grandpa gave me this recipe that his mom baked for him while he was growing up. They are his favorite cookies!

2 cups packed brown sugar
1 cup shortening
1 cup milk
2 eggs
2 teaspoons vanilla extract
3 cups flour
1 teaspoon baking powder
1 teaspoon baking soda
1 teaspoon cinnamon
1 teaspoon nutmeg
1 teaspoon ground cloves
1/2 teaspoon salt
2 cups quick-cooking oats
1 cup raisins, plumped

- Beat the brown sugar, shortening, milk and eggs in a mixer bowl until smooth. Add the vanilla and mix well. Beat in the flour.
- Add the baking powder, baking soda, cinnamon, nutmeg, cloves and salt, beating constantly until blended. Stir in the oats and raisins. Drop by teaspoonfuls onto a nonstick cookie sheet.
- Bake at 375 degrees for 12 minutes.
- Cool on cookie sheet for 2 minutes. Remove to a wire rack to cool completely.
- Yield: 100 servings.

Approx Per Serving: Cal 59; 36% Calories from Fat; T Fat 2 g; Chol 5 mg; Sod 26 mg; Carbo 9 g; Fiber <1 g; Prot 1 g

Caroline Seward, New Providence

OATMEAL COOKIES

I received a blue ribbon at the Jones County Fair with this recipe.

1/2 cup shortening
1/2 cup sugar
1/2 cup packed brown sugar
1 egg
1/4 teaspoon vanilla extract
1 cup flour
1/2 teaspoon baking powder
1/2 teaspoon baking soda
1/2 teaspoon salt
3/4 cup rolled oats

- Beat the shortening, sugar, brown sugar, egg and vanilla in a mixer bowl until creamy. Add the flour, baking powder, baking soda and salt and mix well. Stir in the oats. Drop by teaspoonfuls onto a cookie sheet.
- Bake at 350 degrees for 10 to 12 minutes or until light brown. Cool on cookie sheet for 2 minutes. Remove to a wire rack to cool completely.
- Yield: 36 servings.

Approx Per Serving: Cal 67; 42% Calories from Fat; T Fat 3 g; Chol 6 mg; Sod 49 mg; Carbo 9 g; Fiber <1 g; Prot 1 g

Robin Stolte, Olin

PRIDE-OF-IOWA COOKIES

This is our family's favorite cookie! Pride-of-Iowa Cookies contain so many ingredients which are grown in, or are common to, Iowa—cornflakes, oats, walnuts, butter and eggs. I entered these cookies for a Food and Nutrition project at the fair and won a blue ribbon.

1 cup packed brown sugar
1 cup sugar
1 cup butter, softened
2 eggs
2 cups flour
1 teaspoon baking soda
1 teaspoon baking powder
1/2 teaspoon salt
2 cups quick-cooking oats
2 cups cornflakes
1/2 cup shredded coconut
1/2 cup semisweet chocolate chips
1/2 cup butterscotch chips
1 teaspoon vanilla extract

- Beat the brown sugar, sugar and butter in a mixer bowl until creamy. Add the eggs and mix well. Add a sifted mixture of the flour, baking soda, baking powder and salt, beating until blended.
- Stir in the oats, cornflakes, coconut, chocolate chips, butterscotch chips and vanilla. Drop by spoonfuls onto a greased cookie sheet.
- Bake at 350 degrees for 8 minutes or until light brown.
- Cool on cookie sheet for 2 minutes. Remove to a wire rack to cool completely.
- May add 1/2 cup chopped nuts.
- Yield: 54 servings.

Approx Per Serving: Cal 111; 40% Calories from Fat; T Fat 5 g; Chol 17 mg; Sod 93 mg; Carbo 16 g; Fiber 1 g; Prot 1 g

Christopher Schmidt, Farmersburg

PUMPKIN COOKIES

1 cup shortening
1 cup sugar
1 egg
1 cup mashed cooked pumpkin
1 teaspoon vanilla extract
1 cup chopped dates or raisins
2 cups flour
1 teaspoon baking powder
1 teaspoon baking soda
1 teaspoon cinnamon
1/2 teaspoon salt
1/2 cup packed brown sugar
1/4 cup milk
3 tablespoons butter
1 cup confectioners' sugar
1 teaspoon vanilla extract

- Combine the shortening, sugar, egg, pumpkin, 1 teaspoon vanilla, dates, flour, baking powder, baking soda, cinnamon and salt in the order listed in a mixer bowl and mix well. Drop by tablespoonfuls onto an ungreased cookie sheet.
- Bake at 350 degrees for 10 minutes; bottoms of cookies will be light brown.
- Cool on cookie sheet for 2 minutes. Remove to a wire rack to cool completely.
- Bring the brown sugar, milk and butter to a boil in a saucepan. Boil for 2 minutes, stirring constantly.
- Let stand until cool. Add the confectioners' sugar and 1 teaspoon vanilla and beat until smooth. Spread over the cookies.
- May add 1/2 cup chopped nuts to the cookie dough.
- Yield: 72 servings.

Approx Per Serving: Cal 74; 42% Calories from Fat; T Fat 3 g; Chol 4 mg; Sod 38 mg; Carbo 10 g; Fiber <1 g; Prot 1 g

Valerie Wolter, Dubuque

SUGAR COOKIES

1 cup confectioners' sugar
1 cup sugar
1 cup margarine, softened
1 cup corn oil
2 eggs, beaten
1 teaspoon vanilla extract
4 cups flour
1 teaspoon baking soda
1 teaspoon cream of tartar
1/4 teaspoon salt

- Beat the confectioners' sugar, sugar, margarine, corn oil, eggs and vanilla in a mixer bowl until smooth. Add the flour, baking soda, cream of tartar and salt.
- Beat until blended, scraping the bowl occasionally. Shape into balls. Arrange on a cookie sheet. Flatten each ball with a glass dipped in sugar.
- Bake at 325 degrees for 8 to 10 minutes or until light brown.
- Cool on cookie sheet for 2 minutes. Remove to a wire rack to cool completely.
- Yield: 72 servings.

Approx Per Serving: Cal 94; 55% Calories from Fat; T Fat 6 g; Chol 6 mg; Sod 51 mg; Carbo 10 g; Fiber <1 g; Prot 1 g

Jason Luedtke, Ankeny

MOLASSES SUGAR COOKIES

My grandma, Dorothy, always makes these cookies for me. They are my favorite.

1 cup sugar
3/4 cup melted shortening
1/4 cup dark molasses
1 egg
2 cups flour
2 teaspoons baking soda
1 teaspoon cinnamon
1/2 teaspoon ground cloves
1/2 teaspoon ground ginger
1/2 teaspoon salt
1 cup sugar

- Beat 1 cup sugar, shortening, molasses and egg in a mixer bowl until blended. Add a sifted mixture of the flour, baking soda, cinnamon, cloves, ground ginger and salt and mix well.
- Chill, covered, in the refrigerator. Shape into 1-inch balls. Roll in 1 cup sugar. Arrange 2 inches apart on a greased cookie sheet.
- Bake at 375 degrees for 8 to 10 minutes or until light brown.
- Cool on cookie sheet for 2 minutes. Remove to a wire rack to cool completely.
- Yield: 36 servings.

Approx Per Serving: Cal 113; 35% Calories from Fat; T Fat 4 g; Chol 6 mg; Sod 79 mg; Carbo 18 g; Fiber <1 g; Prot 1 g

Stacy Schlapkohl, Durant

SNOW ON THE MOUNTAIN

2 cups sugar
4 eggs
2 teaspoons vanilla extract
2 1/2 cups flour
1/2 cup melted butter
9 tablespoons baking cocoa
2 teaspoons baking powder
1/2 teaspoon salt
1 cup chopped pecans
1 1/4 cups confectioners' sugar

- Beat the sugar, eggs and vanilla in a mixer bowl until blended. Add the flour, butter, baking cocoa, baking powder and salt and mix well. Stir in the pecans.
- Chill, covered, for 2 hours or until firm. Shape into balls. Roll in confectioners' sugar. Arrange on a cookie sheet.
- Bake at 350 degrees for 10 minutes; do not overbake.
- Yield: 48 servings.

Approx Per Serving: Cal 110; 33% Calories from Fat; T Fat 4 g; Chol 23 mg; Sod 61 mg; Carbo 18 g; Fiber 1 g; Prot 2 g

Katie Winkler, Iowa Falls

Cakes, Pies, and Desserts

Nature's Pyramids

by *Travis Harland*
Marshalltown

"Nature provides food for both the eye and the palate," said Travis Harland of Marshall County. The white dwarf trillium, found in the Harland family woodlands, reminds Travis of the food guide pyramid, which is also triangular in shape. Travis is a member of the Albion Ables 4-H Club and has taken photography for seven years. Travis is the son of Bruce and Bonita Harland.

Cakes • 145

IOWA APPLESAUCE CAKE

For a decorative finish, set a doily lightly on the frosted cake and sprinkle lightly with a mixture of cinnamon and nutmeg, then remove the doily carefully.

1/2 cup butter, margarine or shortening, softened
3/4 cup sugar
3/4 cup packed brown sugar
1 egg
2 cups flour
2 teaspoons baking powder
1 teaspoon baking soda
1 teaspoon cinnamon
1/2 teaspoon ground cloves
1 1/2 cups applesauce
1 cup raisins
1/2 cup chopped walnuts or pecans
Cream Cheese Frosting (below)

- Cream the butter, sugar and brown sugar in a large bowl until light and fluffy.
- Beat in the egg.
- Add a mixture of flour, baking powder, baking soda, cinnamon and cloves alternately with applesauce, mixing well after each addition.
- Stir in the raisins and walnuts. Spread the batter evenly in a greased 9x13-inch cake pan.
- Bake at 350 degrees for 30 to 35 minutes or until the cake tests done.
- Cool in the pan on a wire rack.
- Frost with the Cream Cheese Frosting.
- Refrigerate leftovers.
- Yield: 12 servings.

Approx Per Serving: Cal 610; 35% Calories from Fat; T Fat 24 g; Chol 75 mg; Sod 335 mg; Carbo 98 g; Fiber 2 g; Prot 5 g

Terry E. Branstad, Governor of Iowa

CREAM CHEESE FROSTING

6 ounces cream cheese, softened
1/2 cup butter or margarine, softened
2 teaspoons vanilla extract
4 1/2 to 4 3/4 cups sifted confectioners' sugar

- Beat the cream cheese, butter and vanilla in a bowl until light and fluffy.
- Beat in 2 cups of the confectioners' sugar until smooth. Add enough remaining confectioners' sugar to make of spreading consistency.
- Refrigerate leftovers.

BLACK BOTTOM CUPCAKES

8 ounces cream cheese, softened
1/3 cup sugar
1 egg
1/8 teaspoon salt
1 cup semisweet chocolate chips
1 1/2 cups flour
1/4 cup baking cocoa
1/2 teaspoon salt
1 cup sugar
1 teaspoon baking soda
1 egg
1 cup water
1 tablespoon white vinegar
1/3 cup vegetable oil
1 teaspoon vanilla extract

- Combine the first 4 ingredients in a bowl and beat until smooth and creamy. Stir in the chocolate chips and set aside.
- Sift the flour, baking cocoa, salt, sugar and baking soda into a medium bowl. Add the egg, water, vinegar, oil and vanilla and mix until smooth.
- Fill paper-lined muffin cups half full with the chocolate batter. Add a heaping teaspoonful of the cream cheese mixture in the center.
- Bake at 350 degrees for 25 minutes. Let stand until cool. Store in the refrigerator.
- May sprinkle the tops with a small amount of sugar and chopped almonds before baking if desired.
- Yield: 20 cupcakes.

Approx Per Serving: Cal 208; 45% Calories from Fat; T Fat 11 g; Chol 34 mg; Sod 149 mg; Carbo 27 g; Fiber 1 g; Prot 3 g

Amy Steele, Washington

CHOCOLATE ANGEL FOOD CAKE ❖

I started making a regular angel food cake for 4-H and then decided to try a chocolate angel food cake. The regular one got an outstanding and the chocolate went to the state fair.

2 cups sifted sugar
1 cup cake flour, sifted
1/4 cup baking cocoa
15 egg whites
1/4 teaspoon salt
1 1/2 teaspoons cream of tartar
1 teaspoon vanilla extract
1/4 teaspoon almond extract

- Sift the sugar, flour and baking cocoa together 3 times and set aside.
- Beat the egg whites in a large bowl until frothy. Add the salt and cream of tartar. Beat until stiff peaks form. Beat in the vanilla and almond flavorings.
- Fold in the flour mixture gently.
- Pour into an ungreased tube pan. Bake at 325 degrees for 1 hour.
- Invert the cake on a funnel to cool. Loosen from the side of the pan and invert onto a cake plate.
- May omit the cocoa and add 1/4 cup cake flour.
- Yield: 16 servings.

Approx Per Serving: Cal 93; 10% Calories from Fat; T Fat 1 g; Chol <1 mg; Sod 107 mg; Carbo 18 g; Fiber <1 g; Prot 4 g

Briana Greiner, Harper

Cakes • 147

CHOCOLATE CHERRY CAKE

1 (2-layer) package chocolate cake mix
1 (21-ounce) can cherry pie filling
4 eggs

- Combine the cake mix, pie filling and eggs in a bowl and beat until the cherries are crunched up. Pour into a greased 9x13-inch cake pan.
- Bake at 350 degrees for 30 minutes or until the top springs back when lightly touched.
- Serve warm with vanilla ice cream or frost if desired.
- Yield: 15 servings.

Approx Per Serving: Cal 213; 28% Calories from Fat; T Fat 7 g; Chol 57 mg; Sod 318 mg; Carbo 36 g; Fiber 1 g; Prot 4 g

Staci Sessler, Aplington

CHOCOLATE CHIP CAKE

2¼ cups cake flour
1¾ cups sugar
1 tablespoon baking powder
1 teaspoon salt
½ cup vegetable oil
5 egg yolks
¾ cup cold water
2 teaspoons vanilla extract
1 cup egg whites
½ teaspoon cream of tartar
3 (1-ounce) squares unsweetened chocolate, coarsely grated

- Sift the first 4 ingredients into a large bowl. Make a well in the center.
- Add the oil, unbeaten egg yolks, water and vanilla and beat until smooth.
- Beat the egg whites with cream of tartar in a bowl until stiff peaks form. Fold the stiffly beaten egg whites into the egg yolk mixture gradually. Fold in the grated chocolate.
- Pour the batter into an ungreased tube pan. Bake at 325 degrees for 55 minutes.
- Increase the oven temperature to 350 degrees and bake for 10 to 15 minutes longer.
- Invert the cake on a funnel to cool. Loosen the cake from the side of the pan. Invert onto a cake plate.
- Yield: 16 servings.

Approx Per Serving: Cal 253; 45% Calories from Fat; T Fat 13 g; Chol 67 mg; Sod 269 mg; Carbo 33 g; Fiber 1 g; Prot 4 g

Melanie Spies, Manilla

WACKY CHOCOLATE CAKE

3 cups flour
2 cups sugar
5 tablespoons baking cocoa
2 teaspoons baking soda
1 teaspoon salt
¼ cup vinegar
2 teaspoons vanilla extract
¾ cup vegetable oil
2 cups water
6 tablespoons margarine
6 tablespoons milk
1½ cups sugar
½ cup chocolate chips

- Sift the flour, 2 cups sugar, baking cocoa, baking soda and salt into a bowl. Add the vinegar, vanilla, oil and water and mix well.
- Pour into a greased and floured 9x13-inch cake pan.
- Bake at 350 degrees for 20 to 30 minutes or until the cake tests done.
- Combine the margarine, milk and 1½ cups sugar in a saucepan. Bring to a boil, stirring constantly. Remove from the heat. Add the chocolate chips and stir until melted.
- Spread over the warm cake.
- Yield: 15 servings.

Approx Per Serving: Cal 444; 35% Calories from Fat; T Fat 18 g; Chol 1 mg; Sod 310 mg; Carbo 71 g; Fiber 2 g; Prot 3 g

Jonathan and Allie Follett, Waukee

CREAM CHEESE POUND CAKE

This is my family's favorite cake. I got reserve champion at the county fair with the recipe.

1½ cups butter, softened
8 ounces cream cheese, softened
2⅓ cups sugar
6 eggs, at room temperature
3 cups flour
1 teaspoon vanilla extract

- Cream the butter and cream cheese in a large bowl. Add the sugar gradually and beat for 5 to 7 minutes or until light and fluffy.
- Beat in the eggs 1 at a time.
- Add the flour gradually, beating just until blended after each addition. Stir in the vanilla.
- Pour into a greased and floured 10-inch tube pan.
- Bake at 300 degrees for 1½ hours or until the cake tests done.
- Cool in the pan on a wire rack for 15 minutes. Remove to a wire rack to cool completely.
- Yield: 16 servings.

Approx Per Serving: Cal 428; 51% Calories from Fat; T Fat 24 g; Chol 142 mg; Sod 242 mg; Carbo 48 g; Fiber 1 g; Prot 6 g

Betsy Zeller, Bancroft

Cakes • 149

DATE CAKE

1 cup chopped dates
1 teaspoon baking soda
1 cup boiling water
1 cup sugar
1 tablespoon butter, softened
1 cup flour
1/3 teaspoon salt
2/3 cup sugar
2 tablespoons (heaping) flour
4 cups milk
1 teaspoon vanilla extract
Nutmeg and salt to taste

- Sprinkle the dates with baking soda in a small bowl. Add the boiling water and mix well. Set aside to cool.
- Cream 1 cup sugar and butter in a medium bowl. Add the date mixture, 1 cup flour and 1/3 teaspoon salt and mix well. Pour into a lightly greased 9x9-inch cake pan.
- Bake at 350 degrees for 30 minutes. Cool in the pan on a wire rack.
- Mix 2/3 cup sugar and 2 tablespoons flour in a saucepan. Stir in the milk gradually. Cook until thickened, stirring constantly. Add the vanilla, nutmeg and salt to taste and blend well.
- Serve the cake with the sauce.
- Refrigerate leftovers.
- Yield: 10 servings.

Approx Per Serving: Cal 299; 14% Calories from Fat; T Fat 5 g; Chol 16 mg; Sod 214 mg; Carbo 62 g; Fiber 2 g; Prot 5 g

Charles Goodall, Waukee

PUMPKIN SHEET CAKE

We are often asked to bring these to 4-H meetings or parties. Everyone says this recipe is better than their recipe.

1 (16-ounce) can pumpkin
2 cups sugar
1 cup vegetable oil
4 eggs, lightly beaten
2 cups flour
2 teaspoons baking soda
1 teaspoon cinnamon
1/2 teaspoon salt
3 ounces cream cheese, softened
5 tablespoons butter or margarine, softened
1 teaspoon vanilla extract
1 3/4 cups confectioners' sugar
3 to 4 teaspoons milk

- Combine the pumpkin, sugar and oil in a large bowl and mix well. Beat in the eggs.
- Add a mixture of flour, baking soda, cinnamon and salt and beat until well blended. Pour into a greased 10x15-inch cake pan.
- Bake at 350 degrees for 25 to 30 minutes or until the cake tests done. Cool on a wire rack.
- Beat the cream cheese, butter and vanilla in a small bowl until smooth. Beat in the confectioners' sugar gradually. Beat in enough milk gradually to make the frosting of spreading consistency.
- Frost the cooled cake.
- Refrigerate leftovers.
- Yield: 20 servings.

Approx Per Serving: Cal 324; 45% Calories from Fat; T Fat 17 g; Chol 55 mg; Sod 192 mg; Carbo 42 g; Fiber 1 g; Prot 3 g

Carissa Allen, Promise City

BOILED RAISIN CAKE

This old family recipe was a favorite of my grandfather who loved raisins.

1 cup raisins
½ cup shortening
1½ cups sugar
2 eggs
2 teaspoons cinnamon
¼ teaspoon nutmeg
¼ teaspoon cloves
1 teaspoon baking soda
2 cups flour

- Combine the raisins and enough water to cover generously. Boil the raisins for several minutes and remove from the heat. Drain the raisins, reserving 1 cup of the raisin liquid.
- Cream the shortening and sugar in a large bowl until light and fluffy. Add the eggs and spices and mix well.
- Dissolve the baking soda in the reserved raisin liquid. Add the flour and raisin liquid alternately to the creamed mixture, mixing well after each addition. Stir in the raisins.
- Pour into a greased and floured 9x13-inch cake pan.
- Bake at 350 degrees for 30 minutes or until the cake tests done.
- Cool in the pan on a wire rack.
- Yield: 15 servings.

Approx Per Serving: Cal 241; 28% Calories from Fat; T Fat 8 g; Chol 28 mg; Sod 65 mg; Carbo 41 g; Fiber 1 g; Prot 3 g

Julie Grawe, Strawberry Point

STRAWBERRY CAKE

1 (2-layer) package white cake mix
½ cup water
½ cup vegetable oil
3 eggs
1 (3-ounce) package strawberry gelatin
1 tablespoon flour
½ cup mashed strawberries
8 ounces whipped topping
1 (10-ounce) package frozen strawberries, thawed

- Combine the cake mix, water and oil in a large bowl and mix well. Add the eggs 1 at time, beating well after each addition.
- Mix the dry gelatin, flour and ½ cup strawberries in a small bowl. Add to the cake batter and mix well. Pour into a greased and floured 9x13-inch cake pan.
- Bake at 350 degrees for 35 to 40 minutes or until the cake tests done. Cool in the pan on a wire rack.
- Mix the whipped topping and thawed strawberries in a bowl and spread over the cooled cake. Store in the refrigerator.
- Yield: 15 servings.

Approx Per Serving: Cal 305; 46% Calories from Fat; T Fat 16 g; Chol 42 mg; Sod 257 mg; Carbo 38 g; Fiber 1 g; Prot 4 g

Janelle Tucker, Earlville

WALDORF ASTORIA CAKES

2 cups shortening
6 cups sugar
8 eggs
8 ounces red food coloring
4 teaspoons vanilla extract
8 teaspoons baking cocoa
4 cups buttermilk
9 cups sifted flour
4 teaspoons salt
4 teaspoons vinegar
4 teaspoons baking soda
3 cups cold milk
9 tablespoons flour
3 cups butter, softened
3 cups sugar
1 teaspoon vanilla extract

- Cream the shortening and 6 cups sugar in a large bowl until light and fluffy. Add the eggs and beat for 2 minutes.
- Blend the food coloring, 4 teaspoons vanilla and baking cocoa in a small bowl. Add to the creamed mixture and mix well. Add the buttermilk and 9 cups flour alternately, mixing well after each addition.
- Mix the salt, vinegar and baking soda in a small bowl. Add to the batter while the mixture is still foaming and mix well. Pour the batter into greased and floured layer cake pans.
- Bake at 325 degrees until the layers test done. Cool in the pans on wire racks for 10 minutes. Remove to wire racks to cool completely.
- Combine the milk and 9 tablespoons flour in a large saucepan. Cook until smooth and thickened, stirring constantly. Cool to room temperature.
- Cream the butter, 3 cups sugar and 1 teaspoon vanilla in a large bowl. Add the flour mixture and beat for 20 minutes or until fluffy. Spread the frosting between layers and over the top and sides of cakes.
- Yield: 30 servings.

Approx Per Serving: Cal 701; 44% Calories from Fat; T Fat 35 g; Chol 111 mg; Sod 646 mg; Carbo 91 g; Fiber 1 g; Prot 8 g

Seven Villages Restaurant, Williamsburg

BISHOPS CHOCOLATE PIE

1 (4-ounce) package French vanilla instant pudding mix
1 (4-ounce) package chocolate fudge instant pudding mix
2 cups milk
2 cups vanilla ice cream, softened
1 graham cracker pie shell
8 ounces whipped topping
2 ounces milk chocolate

- Beat the pudding mixes and milk in a bowl until smooth. Add the ice cream and blend well.
- Pour into the pie shell. Spread with whipped topping.
- Shave the chocolate with a vegetable peeler to make curls. Arrange the chocolate curls on top.
- Yield: 8 servings.

Approx Per Serving: Cal 520; 43% Calories from Fat; T Fat 25 g; Chol 25 mg; Sod 656 mg; Carbo 70 g; Fiber 2 g; Prot 6 g

Kati Peiffer, Washington

APPLE PIE

I won a purple ribbon with this pie and it was chosen to go to the state fair.

3/4 cup sugar
1/4 cup flour
1/2 teaspoon each nutmeg and cinnamon
1/8 teaspoon salt
6 cups sliced peeled apples
Grandma's Pie Pastry (below)
2 tablespoons butter
1 teaspoon sugar

- Mix 3/4 cup sugar, flour, spices and salt in a large bowl. Add the apples and toss to coat.
- Line a 9-inch pie plate with 1 pastry circle. Add the apple mixture. Dot with butter.
- Top with the remaining pastry, sealing edge and cutting vents. Sprinkle with 1 teaspoon sugar. Cover edge with foil to prevent overbrowning.
- Bake at 425 degrees for 25 minutes. Remove foil. Bake for 15 minutes longer or until the crust is brown and juice begins to bubble through the vents.
- Yield: 8 servings.

Approx Per Serving: Cal 429; 43% Calories from Fat; T Fat 21 g; Chol 24 mg; Sod 263 mg; Carbo 58 g; Fiber 3 g; Prot 4 g

Matt Rohrig, Orient

GRANDMA'S PIE PASTRY

2 cups flour
3/4 teaspoon salt
2/3 cup lard
5 tablespoons cold water
2 teaspoons vinegar

- Mix the flour and salt in a bowl. Cut in the lard until crumbly.
- Sprinkle with a mixture of water and vinegar 1 tablespoon at a time, mixing until moistened and the dough almost cleans the side of the bowl.
- Divide into 2 portions and shape each into a ball. Roll each ball into a circle on a lightly floured surface.

Matt Rohrig, Orient

SUGAR-FREE BANANA CREAM PIE

1 small package sugar-free banana instant pudding mix
2 bananas, sliced
1 baked (8-inch) pie shell
8 ounces fat-free whipped topping

- Prepare the pudding mix using the package directions.
- Arrange half the banana slices in the pie shell. Pour the pudding over the bananas.
- Spread the whipped topping over the pudding and arrange the remaining banana slices on top.
- Chill for 5 to 10 minutes and serve immediately.
- Yield: 6 servings.

Approx Per Serving: Cal 296; 38% Calories from Fat; T Fat 12 g; Chol 11 mg; Sod 295 mg; Carbo 40 g; Fiber 1 g; Prot 5 g

Anthony Sherwood-Pollard, Lenox

GRANDMA DOROTHY'S CHOCOLATE CHIP PIE

10 graham crackers, crushed
1/4 cup melted butter
1/2 cup milk
28 to 30 large marshmallows
1 cup whipped cream
1 teaspoon vanilla extract
2 ounces bittersweet chocolate, grated

- Mix the cracker crumbs and butter in a bowl. Press over the bottom and side of a 9-inch pie plate. Set aside.
- Heat the milk in a saucepan. Add the marshmallows and heat until the marshmallows melt, stirring frequently. Remove from heat and let stand until cool.
- Fold in the whipped cream, vanilla and chocolate. Pour into the prepared pie plate.
- Chill for several hours or until firm.
- Yield: 8 servings.

Approx Per Serving: Cal 318; 57% Calories from Fat; T Fat 21 g; Chol 58 mg; Sod 143 mg; Carbo 33 g; Fiber <1 g; Prot 3 g

Shelby Jensen, Exira

GREAT-GRANDMA BETTY'S CUSTARD PIE

1 unbaked (9-inch) pie shell
2 1/2 cups milk, scalded, cooled
4 eggs
1/2 cup sugar
1/8 teaspoon salt
1 teaspoon vanilla extract

- Bake the pie shell at 350 degrees for 3 minutes. Let stand until cool.
- Combine the milk with the remaining ingredients and beat until blended. Pour into the partially baked pie shell.
- Bake at 325 degrees for 40 minutes or until the center is almost set but still soft. The center will set as the pie cools. Refrigerate until serving time.
- Yield: 6 servings.

Approx Per Serving: Cal 334; 46% Calories from Fat; T Fat 17 g; Chol 155 mg; Sod 299 mg; Carbo 36 g; Fiber 1 g; Prot 9 g

Molly Lytle, Harlan

SUGAR-FREE CHOCOLATE PEANUT BUTTER PIE

1 small package sugar-free chocolate instant pudding mix
3 tablespoons peanut butter
1 baked (8-inch) pie shell
8 ounces fat-free whipped topping
1/4 cup chopped unsalted peanuts

- Prepare the pudding mix using the package directions and stir in the peanut butter.
- Pour into the cooled pie shell. Spread with the whipped topping and sprinkle with peanuts.
- Chill for 5 to 10 minutes or until set.
- Yield: 6 servings.

Approx Per Serving: Cal 430; 52% Calories from Fat; T Fat 25 g; Chol 6 mg; Sod 481 mg; Carbo 40 g; Fiber 3 g; Prot 12 g

Kiley Sherwood-Pollard, Lenox

PEANUT BUTTER PIE

This pie won a purple ribbon in "Promote Our Commodities" at the 1996 fair.

20 chocolate cookies, crushed
1/4 cup sugar
1/4 cup melted butter
8 ounces cream cheese, softened
1 cup creamy peanut butter
1 cup sugar
1 tablespoon butter, softened
1 teaspoon vanilla extract
1 cup whipping cream, whipped

- Measure 1 1/4 cups cookie crumbs and mix with 1/4 cup sugar and melted butter. Press over the bottom and side of a 9-inch pie plate.
- Bake at 375 degrees for 10 minutes. Cool.
- Combine the cream cheese, peanut butter, 1 cup sugar, 1 tablespoon butter and vanilla in a bowl and beat until creamy. Fold in the whipped cream gently. Pour into the prepared pie plate.
- Garnish with grated chocolate or additional chocolate crumbs. Chill until serving time.
- Yield: 8 servings.

Approx Per Serving: Cal 617; 64% Calories from Fat; T Fat 46 g; Chol 92 mg; Sod 378 mg; Carbo 47 g; Fiber 2 g; Prot 11 g

Jennifer Huntington, Geneva

CLASSIC PECAN PIE

3 eggs, lightly beaten
1 cup light or dark corn syrup
1 cup sugar
2 tablespoons melted margarine
1 teaspoon vanilla extract
1 1/2 cups pecans
1 unbaked (9-inch) pie shell

- Combine the eggs, corn syrup, sugar, margarine and vanilla in a bowl and mix until well blended. Stir in the pecans. Pour into the pie shell.
- Bake at 350 degrees for 50 minutes or until a knife inserted halfway between the center and edge comes out clean.
- Yield: 8 servings.

Approx Per Serving: Cal 519; 44% Calories from Fat; T Fat 26 g; Chol 80 mg; Sod 229 mg; Carbo 71 g; Fiber 2 g; Prot 5 g

Mindy Jorgensen, Osceola

GREEN TOMATO PIE

1 1/3 cups sugar
6 2/3 tablespoons flour
1 1/3 teaspoons salt
1 1/3 teaspoons cinnamon
4 cups chopped green tomatoes
1/4 cup lemon juice
1/3 to 1/2 cup raisins, plumped, drained
1 recipe (2-crust) pie pastry
2 tablespoons (about) butter

- Combine the sugar, flour, salt and cinnamon in a saucepan. Add the tomatoes and toss to mix. Add the lemon juice and raisins.
- Bring the mixture just to a boil over medium heat.
- Spoon the mixture into a pastry-lined 9-inch pie plate. Dot with butter. Top with the remaining pastry, sealing edge and cutting vents.
- Bake at 375 degrees for 35 to 45 minutes or until golden brown.
- Yield: 8 servings.

Approx Per Serving: Cal 443; 34% Calories from Fat; T Fat 17 g; Chol 8 mg; Sod 615 mg; Carbo 71 g; Fiber 3 g; Prot 5 g

Cassie Osborn, Casey

FLAKY PIE PASTRY

4 cups flour
1 tablespoon sugar
2 teaspoons salt
1 3/4 cups shortening
1 egg, beaten
1/2 cup water
1 tablespoon vinegar

- Measure the flour by spooning lightly into the measuring cup. Combine the flour, sugar and salt in a bowl. Cut in the shortening until crumbly.
- Beat the egg with water and vinegar in a bowl. Add to the flour mixture and mix with a fork until moistened. Divide into 5 portions and shape each into a flat round patty. Wrap each in plastic wrap and chill for 30 minutes or longer.
- Sprinkle flour lightly on each side of each portion. Roll each portion on a lightly floured surface into a 1/8-inch-thick circle 2 inches larger than an inverted pie plate. Fold into halves or quarters. Place in a pie plate and fit loosely into the pie plate, pressing gently to remove air pockets and crimping edge decoratively.
- Use pie shells as instructed in individual recipes. Pie shells freeze well.
- Yield: 5 pie shells.

Approx Per Shell: Cal 1023; 65% Calories from Fat; T Fat 74 g; Chol 42 mg; Sod 867 mg; Carbo 79 g; Fiber 3 g; Prot 12 g

Candy Abbott, Webster City

APPLE COBBLER

1 (10-pound) can sliced apples
1½ cups sugar
¼ cup lemon juice
2 tablespoons vanilla extract
3 tablespoons tapioca
1 tablespoon cinnamon
4 cups flour
2 cups packed brown sugar
½ cup plus 3 tablespoons butter

- Combine the apples, sugar, lemon juice, vanilla, tapioca and cinnamon in a large bowl and mix well. Spread evenly in a shallow 7½-quart baking pan.
- Mix the flour and brown sugar in a bowl. Cut in the butter until crumbly. Spread over the apple mixture.
- Bake at 325 degrees for 45 to 55 minutes or until golden brown. Serve warm or let stand until completely cool before covering with foil.
- Yield: 24 servings.

Approx Per Serving: Cal 363; 15% Calories from Fat; T Fat 6 g; Chol 14 mg; Sod 66 mg; Carbo 77 g; Fiber 4 g; Prot 3 g

Landmark Restaurant, Williamsburg

MICROWAVED APPLE STREUSEL

3 cups sliced peeled apples
¾ cup packed brown sugar
½ cup flour
⅓ cup packed brown sugar
⅓ cup rolled oats
½ teaspoon cinnamon
¼ cup butter

- Place the apples in a 9x13-inch glass baking dish. Sprinkle with ¾ cup brown sugar.
- Mix flour, ⅓ cup brown sugar, oats and cinnamon in a bowl. Cut in the butter until crumbly. Spread over the apples.
- Microwave on High for 9 to 10 minutes or until the apples are tender.
- Yield: 6 servings.

Approx Per Serving: Cal 277; 26% Calories from Fat; T Fat 8 g; Chol 21 mg; Sod 91 mg; Carbo 51 g; Fiber 2 g; Prot 2 g

Kara Donaldson, Osceola

BANANA DESSERT

2 cups crushed vanilla wafers
½ cup butter, softened
1½ cups confectioners' sugar
½ cup egg substitute
3 (or more) bananas, sliced
12 ounces whipped topping

- Reserve a small amount of the crumbs for topping. Spread the remaining crumbs over the bottom of an 8x10-inch dish.
- Cream the butter and confectioners' sugar in a bowl. Beat in the egg substitute. Spread over the crumbs.
- Cover the confectioners' sugar mixture with banana slices. Spread the whipped topping over the bananas, covering completely. Sprinkle the reserved crumbs over the top.
- Chill for several hours.
- Yield: 8 servings.

Approx Per Serving: Cal 434; 49% Calories from Fat; T Fat 26 g; Chol 44 mg; Sod 225 mg; Carbo 58 g; Fiber 1 g; Prot 4 g

Amanda Fett, Northwood

CALIFORNIA DESSERT

1 (2-layer) package chocolate cake mix
4 (5-ounce) cans prepared chocolate fudge pudding
16 ounces whipped topping

- Prepare and bake the cake mix using the package directions for a 9x13-inch cake pan. Cool completely.
- Select a large round glass bowl. Cut 2 circles of cake to fit the bowl. Line the bowl with 2 cans of pudding using a spatula. Place 1 cake circle in the prepared bowl. Cover with half the whipped topping and 1 can pudding.
- Add layers of the remaining cake, remaining pudding and remaining whipped topping. Garnish with chocolate curls. Chill until serving time.
- Yield: 16 servings.

Approx Per Serving: Cal 295; 43% Calories from Fat; T Fat 15 g; Chol 29 mg; Sod 347 mg; Carbo 40 g; Fiber 1 g; Prot 4 g

Billy Joe Travis, Spirit Lake

CREAM PUFF DESSERT

I sometimes make this with sugar-free pudding and my grandpa who is diabetic can enjoy it, too.

1 cup water
½ cup margarine
1 cup flour
4 eggs
1 (6-ounce) package vanilla instant pudding mix
3 cups milk
8 ounces cream cheese, softened
8 ounces whipped topping

- Bring the water and margarine to a boil in a saucepan. Add the flour and beat until the mixture forms a ball. Remove from the heat. Add the eggs 1 at a time, beating well after each addition.
- Spread the mixture in a greased 9x13-inch baking pan. Bake at 400 degrees for 30 minutes. Cool completely.
- Combine the pudding mix, milk and cream cheese in a bowl and beat until smooth. Spread over the cream puff layer. Top with the whipped topping. Garnish with a drizzle of chocolate syrup if desired.
- Chill until serving time.
- Yield: 15 servings.

Approx Per Serving: Cal 277; 59% Calories from Fat; T Fat 18 g; Chol 80 mg; Sod 324 mg; Carbo 23 g; Fiber <1 g; Prot 6 g

Julie Renee Carroll, Avoca

TAFFY APPLE PIZZA

1 (20-ounce) package refrigerated sugar cookie dough
16 ounces fat-free cream cheese, softened
1 cup packed brown sugar
1 teaspoon vanilla extract
5 medium apples
½ cup water
1 tablespoon lemon juice
¼ cup fat-free caramel ice cream topping

- Pat the cookie dough over the bottom of an ungreased deep-dish pizza pan. Bake at 350 degrees for 11 to 14 minutes or until light brown. Let stand until cool.
- Combine the cream cheese, brown sugar and vanilla in a bowl and beat until smooth. Spread over the cooled cookie crust.
- Peel, core and slice the apples. Dip the slices in a mixture of water and lemon juice to prevent browning. Arrange the slices on the cream cheese mixture.
- Drizzle the caramel topping over the top. Cut into wedges with a pizza cutter.
- Yield: 16 servings.

Approx Per Serving: Cal 259; 26% Calories from Fat; T Fat 7 g; Chol 15 mg; Sod 333 mg; Carbo 42 g; Fiber 1 g; Prot 6 g

Amy M. Rappenecker, Sperry

FRUIT PIZZA

1 1/2 cups flour
1/2 cup confectioners' sugar
3/4 cup butter, softened
8 ounces cream cheese, softened
1/2 cup sugar
1 teaspoon vanilla extract
2 cups assorted bite-size apple, banana and peach pieces
1/2 cup sugar
1 tablespoon cornstarch
1 cup orange juice
1 teaspoon lemon juice

- Combine the flour, confectioners' sugar and butter in a bowl and mix until the mixture clings together. Press over the bottom of a 12-inch pizza pan. Bake at 300 degrees for 12 minutes or until light brown. Let stand for 30 minutes or until cool.
- Combine the cream cheese, 1/2 cup sugar and vanilla in a bowl and beat until smooth and creamy. Spread over the cooled crust. Arrange the fruit over the cream cheese mixture.
- Combine the 1/2 cup sugar, cornstarch and juices in a small saucepan. Cook over medium heat until thickened, stirring constantly. Let stand until cool. Spoon over the fruit.
- Chill until serving time. Cut into wedges.
- Yield: 12 servings.

Approx Per Serving: Cal 332; 49% Calories from Fat; T Fat 18 g; Chol 52 mg; Sod 174 mg; Carbo 40 g; Fiber 1 g; Prot 3 g

Mary M. Schiefen, Hawarden

DESSERT PIZZA

1 (6 1/2-ounce) package pizza crust mix
2 teaspoons sugar
1/2 cup hot water
1/4 cup flour
3/4 cup packed brown sugar
3/4 cup rolled oats
1/4 cup melted butter
1 (21-ounce) can apple pie filling
1 cup confectioners' sugar
1 tablespoon water

- Prepare the pizza mix, sugar and hot water using the package directions. Let the dough rest.
- Mix the flour, brown sugar and oats in a bowl. Add the butter and mix until crumbly.
- Pat the dough into a pizza pan. Cover the dough with pie filling. Sprinkle with the oat mixture.
- Bake at 450 degrees for 12 to 17 minutes or until golden brown. Let stand until cool.
- Blend the confectioners' sugar with 1 tablespoon water in a bowl. Drizzle over the pizza.
- May substitute your favorite pie filling for the apple pie filling.
- Yield: 8 servings.

Approx Per Serving: Cal 376; 17% Calories from Fat; T Fat 7 g; Chol 16 mg; Sod 269 mg; Carbo 76 g; Fiber 2 g; Prot 4 g

Stacie Hammen, Harper

PEACH CRISP

3 cups canned peaches
1 cup flour
½ cup sugar
⅓ cup butter

- Pour the peaches into a greased 8-inch square baking pan.
- Mix the flour and sugar in a bowl. Cut in the butter until crumbly. Sprinkle over the peaches.
- Bake at 400 degrees for 30 to 40 minutes or until golden brown. Serve with ice cream if desired.
- Yield: 6 servings.

Approx Per Serving: Cal 325; 28% Calories from Fat; T Fat 11 g; Chol 28 mg; Sod 112 mg; Carbo 58 g; Fiber 2 g; Prot 3 g

Meredith Geschke, New Hampton

FUDGE PUDDING

2 cups flour
1½ cups sugar
½ teaspoon salt
¼ cup baking cocoa
4 teaspoons baking powder
¼ cup melted shortening
1 cup milk
1 cup sugar
1 cup packed brown sugar
½ cup baking cocoa
3½ cups hot water

- Combine the flour, 1½ cups sugar, salt, ¼ cup baking cocoa and baking powder in a bowl. Add the shortening and milk and beat until smooth. Spread in a greased 9x13-inch baking pan.
- Sprinkle a mixture of 1 cup sugar, brown sugar and ½ cup baking cocoa over the batter. Drizzle the hot water over the top.
- Bake at 350 degrees for 45 minutes.
- Let stand for 1 hour before serving. Cut into portions and invert onto dessert plates so that the sauce is on the top.
- Yield: 18 servings.

Approx Per Serving: Cal 239; 14% Calories from Fat; T Fat 4 g; Chol 2 mg; Sod 144 mg; Carbo 51 g; Fiber 1 g; Prot 3 g

Jared Willis, Aplington

RICE PUDDING ❖

½ cup uncooked rice
½ cup sugar
⅛ teaspoon salt
Cinnamon to taste
4 cups milk

- Combine the rice, sugar, salt and cinnamon in a bowl. Stir in 3 cups of the milk. Spoon into a baking dish.
- Bake at 350 degrees for 30 minutes, stirring occasionally.
- Stir in the remaining 1 cup milk. Bake for 30 minutes longer or until the rice is tender.
- Yield: 8 servings.

Approx Per Serving: Cal 165; 23% Calories from Fat; T Fat 4 g; Chol 17 mg; Sod 94 mg; Carbo 27 g; Fiber <1 g; Prot 5 g

Michael Goodall, Waukee

RHUBARB DESSERT

4 eggs
2 cups sugar
1/4 cup flour
6 cups chopped rhubarb
2 cups packed brown sugar
1 1/2 cups flour
10 tablespoons butter

- Beat the eggs in a large bowl. Add the sugar and 1/4 cup flour and mix until smooth. Stir in the rhubarb. Pour into a greased 9x13-inch baking pan.
- Mix the brown sugar and 1 1/2 cups flour in a bowl. Add the butter and mix until crumbly. Sprinkle over the rhubarb mixture.
- Bake at 375 degrees for 30 minutes or until the rhubarb is tender and the topping is golden brown.
- Yield: 15 servings.

Approx Per Serving: Cal 345; 24% Calories from Fat; T Fat 9 g; Chol 77 mg; Sod 107 mg; Carbo 64 g; Fiber 2 g; Prot 4 g

Jason Willis, Aplington

S'MORES-ON-A-GRILL

Graham crackers
Large marshmallows
Milk chocolate candy bars

- Separate the graham crackers into squares. Place a marshmallow on a graham cracker square, add a square of candy and top with another graham cracker. Place in a large foil pie plate.
- Repeat until the pie plate is full. Cover the pie plate with a lid or a sheet of foil. Place the pie plate on a preheated grill rack.
- Heat until the marshmallows and chocolate are melted. Be sure to check frequently and use a hot pad when removing the pie plate from the heat.
- Yield: variable.

Nutritional information for this recipe is not available.

Tresa Clemens, Delta

VANILLA ICE CREAM

1 cup egg substitute
2 cups (scant) sugar
1/8 teaspoon salt
1 1/2 teaspoons (or more) vanilla extract
1 cup whipping cream or half-and-half
4 cups (about) milk

- Beat the egg substitute in a bowl. Add the sugar, salt, vanilla and whipping cream and mix well. Pour into a 1-gallon ice cream freezer container.
- Add enough milk to fill the freezer 2/3 full. Freeze using the manufacturer's directions.
- Yield: 24 servings.

Approx Per Serving: Cal 133; 36% Calories from Fat; T Fat 5 g; Chol 19 mg; Sod 54 mg; Carbo 19 g; Fiber 0 g; Prot 3 g

C. J. Gauger, Ames

TOFFEE REFRIGERATOR DESSERT

2 cups graham cracker crumbs
1 cup soda cracker crumbs
1/2 cup butter, softened
2 (3-ounce) packages vanilla instant pudding mix
2 cups milk
1 quart vanilla ice cream, softened
8 ounces whipped topping
2 (2-ounce) Butterfinger candy bars, frozen

- Mix the cracker crumbs together in a bowl. Add the butter and mix until crumbly. Press over the bottom of a 9x12-inch dish.
- Combine the pudding mix, milk and ice cream in a bowl and mix until well blended. Pour into the prepared dish. Chill until firm.
- Spread whipped topping over the pudding mixture. Crush the candy bars and sprinkle over the top.
- Chill for 2 hours or longer. Store, covered, in the refrigerator.
- Yield: 15 servings.

Approx Per Serving: Cal 367; 45% Calories from Fat; T Fat 19 g; Chol 37 mg; Sod 480 mg; Carbo 47 g; Fiber 1 g; Prot 5 g

Rachel Hustedt, Storm Lake

FUDGE TOPPING FOR ICE CREAM ❖

1 cup sugar
1/4 teaspoon salt
3 tablespoons baking cocoa
3 tablespoons cornstarch
1 tablespoon light corn syrup
1 cup boiling water
1 tablespoon butter
1 teaspoon vanilla extract

- Mix the sugar, salt, baking cocoa and cornstarch in a saucepan. Add the corn syrup and boiling water and mix well.
- Cook until thickened, stirring constantly. Remove from the heat. Add the butter and vanilla.
- Let stand until cool.
- Yield: 20 servings.

Approx Per Serving: Cal 53; 17% Calories from Fat; T Fat 1 g; Chol 2 mg; Sod 34 mg; Carbo 12 g; Fiber 3 g; Prot <1 g

Danika Rasmussen, Hamlin

What's the Best Nutrition Advice?

It's following the Dietary Guidelines for Americans. These are seven guidelines for a healthful diet—advice for healthy Americans two years of age or more. By following the Dietary Guidelines, you can enjoy better health and reduce your chances of getting certain diseases. These Guidelines, developed jointly by USDA and HHS, are the best, most up-to-date advice from nutrition scientists and are the basis of Federal nutrition policy.

The Dietary Guidelines for Americans

- **Eat a variety of foods** to get the energy, protein, vitamins, minerals, and fiber you need for good health.
- **Maintain healthy weight** to reduce your chances of having high blood pressure, heart disease, a stroke, certain cancers, and the most common kind of diabetes.
- **Choose a diet low in fat, saturated fat, and cholesterol** to reduce your risk of heart attack and certain types of cancer. Because fat contains over twice the calories of an equal amount of carbohydrates or protein, a diet low in fat can help you maintain a healthy weight.
- **Choose a diet with plenty of vegetables, fruits, and grain products** which provide needed vitamins, minerals, fiber, and complex carbohydrates and can help you lower your intake of fat.
- **Use sugars only in moderation**. A diet with lots of sugars has too many calories and too few nutrients for most people and can contribute to tooth decay.
- **Use salt and sodium only in moderation** to help reduce your risk of high blood pressure.
- **If you drink alcoholic beverages, do so in moderation**. Alcoholic beverages supply calories, but little or no nutrients. Drinking alcohol is also the cause of many health problems and accidents and can lead to addiction.

Source materials are from the Human Nutrition Information Service—USDA Home and Garden Bulletin Number 252.

Food Guide Pyramid

A Guide to Daily Food Choices

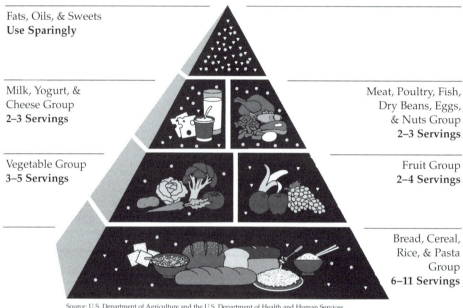

Fats, Oils, & Sweets
Use Sparingly

Milk, Yogurt, & Cheese Group
2–3 Servings

Meat, Poultry, Fish, Dry Beans, Eggs, & Nuts Group
2–3 Servings

Vegetable Group
3–5 Servings

Fruit Group
2–4 Servings

Bread, Cereal, Rice, & Pasta Group
6–11 Servings

Source: U.S. Department of Agriculture and the U.S. Department of Health and Human Services.

Key

● Fat (naturally occurring and added)
▼ Sugars (added)

These symbols show fat and added sugars in foods. They come mostly from the fats, oils, and sweets group. But foods in other groups—such as cheese or ice cream from the milk group or French fries from the vegetable group—can also provide fat and added sugars.

Looking at the Pieces of the Pyramid

The Food Guide Pyramid emphasizes foods from the five major food groups shown in the three lower sections of the Pyramid. Each of these food groups provides some, but not all, of the nutrients you need. Foods in one group cannot replace those in another. No one of these major food groups is more important than another—for good health, you need them all.

Making the Pyramid Work

How Many Servings are Right for Me?
The Pyramid shows a range of servings for each major food group. The number of servings that are right for you depends on how many calories you need, which in turn depends on your age, sex, size, and how active you are. Almost everyone should have at least the lowest number of servings in the ranges.

The following calorie level suggestions are based on recommendations of the National Academy of Sciences and on calorie intakes reported by people in national food consumption surveys.

For Adults and Teens
1,600 calories is about right for many sedentary women and some older adults.

2,200 calories is about right for most children, teenage girls, active women, and many sedentary men. Women who are pregnant or breastfeeding may need somewhat more.

2,800 calories is about right for teenage boys, many active men, and some very active women.

For Young Children
It is hard to know how much food children need to grow normally. If you're unsure, check with your doctor. Preschool children need the same variety of foods as older family members do, but may need less than 1,600 calories. For fewer calories they can eat smaller servings. However, it is important that they have the equivalent of 2 cups of milk a day.

For You
Now, take a look at the table below. It tells you how many servings you need for your calorie level. For example, if you are an active woman who needs about 2,200 calories a day, 9 servings of breads, cereals, rice, or pasta would be right for you. You'd also want to eat about 6 ounces of meat or alternates per day. Keep total fat (fat in the foods you choose as well as fat used in cooking or added at the table) to about 73 grams per day.

If you are between calorie categories, estimate servings. For example, some less active women may need only 2,000 calories to maintain a healthy weight. At that calorie level, 8 servings of breads would be about right.

Sample Diets for a Day at 3 Calorie Levels

	Lower about 1,600	Moderate about 2,200	Higher about 2,800
Bread Group Servings	6	9	11
Vegetable Group Servings	3	4	5
Fruit Group Servings	2	3	4
Milk Group Servings	2–3	2–3	2–3
Meat Group (ounces)	5	6	7
Total Fat (grams)	53	73	93
Total Added Sugars (teaspoons)	6	12	18

What Is a Serving?

The amount of food that counts as a serving is listed below. If you eat a larger portion, count it as more than one serving. For example, 1/2 cup of cooked pasta counts as one serving in the bread, cereal, rice, and pasta group. If you eat 1 cup of pasta, that would be two servings. If you eat a smaller portion, count it as part of a serving.

Isn't 6 to 11 Servings of Bread and Cereals a Lot?

It may sound like a lot, but it's really not. For example, a slice of bread is one serving, so a sandwich for lunch would equal two servings. A small bowl of cereal and one slice of toast for breakfast are two more servings. And, if you have a cup of rice or pasta at dinner, that's two more servings. A snack of 3 or 4 small plain crackers adds yet another serving. So now you've had 7 servings. It adds up quicker than you think!

Do I Need to Measure Servings?

No. Use servings only as a general guide. For mixed foods, do the best you can to estimate the food group servings of the main ingredients. For example, a generous serving of pizza would count in the bread group (crust), the milk group (cheese), and the vegetable group (tomato); a helping of beef stew would count in the meat group and the vegetable group. Both have some fat—fat in the cheese on the pizza and in the gravy from the stew, if it's made from meat drippings.

What If I Want to Lose Weight?

The best and simplest way to lose weight is to increase your physical activity and reduce the fat and sugars in your diet. But be sure to eat at least the lowest number of servings from the five major food groups in the Food Guide Pyramid. You need them for the vitamins, minerals, carbohydrates, and protein they provide. Just try to pick the lowest fat choices from the food groups.

What Counts as a Serving?

Bread, Cereal, Rice, and Pasta
1 slice bread
1 ounce ready-to-eat cereal
1/2 cup cooked cereal, rice, or pasta

Vegetables
1 cup raw leafy vegetables
1/2 cup other vegetables, cooked or chopped raw
3/4 cup vegetable juice

Fruit
1 medium apple, banana, orange
1/2 cup chopped, cooked, or canned fruit and 3/4 cup fruit juice

Milk, Yogurt, and Cheese
1 cup milk or yogurt
1 1/2 ounces natural cheese
2 ounces process cheese

Meat, Poultry, Fish, Dry Beans, Eggs, and Nuts
2 to 3 ounces cooked lean meat, poultry, or fish
1/2 cup cooked dry beans, 1 egg, or 2 tablespoons peanut butter count as 1 ounce lean meat

Index

ACCOMPANIMENTS
  Aletha's Salsa, 77
  Clara's Picante Sauce, 76
  Grandma's Sweet
    Pickles, 77

APPETIZERS. *See also* Dips
  Beef Jerky, 12
  Cheese Balls, 11
  Cheese Puff, 13
  Cheese Spread, 11
  Hidden Valley
    Pinwheels, 14
  Mexican Fudge, 13
  Nacho Platter, 15
  Pick a Pickle, 12
  Stuffed Pizza Bread, 16
  Veg-et Pockets, 16

APPLE
  Apple Cobbler, 156
  Apple Pie, 152
  Apple Salad, 35
  Caramel Apple Salad, 36
  Heart-Healthy Apple
    Coffee Cake, 90
  Iowa Applesauce Cake, 145
  Microwaved Apple
    Streusel, 156
  Taffy Apple Pizza, 158

BEEF
  Dr Pepper Beef Stew, 29
  Fabulous Fajitas, 109
  Football Stew, 30
  Korean Beef, 109
  Potatoes and Cream, 110
  Roast on the Grill, 111
  Shepherd's Pie, 108
  The Cattleman, 110

BEVERAGES, COLD
  Angel Frost, 23
  Banana Yogurt Drink, 24
  Berry Banana Smoothie, 24
  Fruit Smoothie, 24
  Orange Frosty, 25
  Slushy Fruities, 25

BEVERAGES, HOT
  Gourmet Flavored Cocoa
    Mix, 26
  Hot Buttered Ice Cream
    Mix, 25
  Mocha Instant Mix, 26
  Wassail, 87

BEVERAGES, LOW-FAT
  Angel Frost, 23
  Banana Yogurt Drink, 24
  Berry Banana Smoothie, 24
  Fruit Smoothie, 24
  Gourmet Flavored Cocoa
    Mix, 26
  Mocha Instant Mix, 26
  Slushy Fruities, 25
  Wassail, 87

BREADS
  Fry Bread, 51
  Holiday French Toast, 91
  Jiffy Almond Pan Pizza, 54
  Pepperoni Bread, 55
  Swedish Pancakes, 52

BREADS, BREAD MACHINE
  Caramel Nut Rolls in a
    Bread Machine, 55
  Carrot-Dill Bread in a
    Bread Machine, 56
  Oatmeal Bread in a Bread
    Machine, 56

BREADS, LOAVES
  Banana Bread, 49
  Cinnamon Loaf, 49
  Moist and Spicy Pumpkin
    Bread, 50
  Pumpkin Bread, 50
  The Best Rhubarb
    Bread, 51

BREADS, LOW-FAT
  Bran Muffins, 48
  Brooklyn Bagels, 60
  Carrot-Dill Bread in a
    Bread Machine, 56
  Christmas T-Braids, 89
  Cinnamon Loaf, 49
  Coffee Can Wheat
    Bread, 57
  Finnish Bread, 61
  Heart-Healthy Apple
    Coffee Cake, 90
  Moist and Spicy Pumpkin
    Bread, 50
  Oatmeal Bread in a Bread
    Machine, 56
  Pineapple Buns, 90
  Pioneer White Bread, 59
  Shambaugh's Prize
    Bread, 60
  Spicy Low-Fat Apple
    Muffins, 47
  Swedish Pancakes, 52
  White Bread, 59
  Zoete Broodges (Dutch
    Sweet Rolls), 91

BREADS, MUFFINS
  Berry Cream Muffins, 47
  Bran Muffins, 48
  Rhubarb or Apple
    Muffins, 48
  Spicy Low-Fat Apple
    Muffins, 47

BREADS, SWEET
  Birthday Morning
    Cinnamon Rolls, 88
  Bubble Bread, 53
  Butterscotch Rolls, 87
  Christmas T-Braids, 89
  Cream Cheese Coffee
    Cake, 54
  Heart-Healthy Apple
    Coffee Cake, 90
  Monkey Bread, 52
  Orange Poppy Seed
    Scones, 53
  Pineapple Buns, 90
  Zoete Broodges (Dutch
    Sweet Rolls), 91

BREADS, YEAST
  Brooklyn Bagels, 60
  Cheese Snack Bread, 57
  Coffee Can Wheat
    Bread, 57
  Finnish Bread, 61
  Kolaches, 61
  Marble Swirl Bread, 58
  Pioneer White Bread, 59
  Potato Refrigerator
    Rolls, 62
  Seventy-Five-Minute
    Rolls, 62
  Shambaugh's Prize
    Bread, 60
  White Bread, 59

BROCCOLI
  Broccoli Casserole, 66
  Broccoli Cheese
    Casserole, 66

CAKES
  Black Bottom
    Cupcakes, 146
  Boiled Raisin Cake, 150
  Chocolate Angel Food
    Cake, 146
  Chocolate Cherry Cake, 147
  Chocolate Chip Cake, 147
  Cream Cheese Pound
    Cake, 148
  Date Cake, 149
  Dutch Almond Torte, 98

Iowa Applesauce Cake, 145
Pumpkin Sheet Cake, 149
Strawberry Cake, 150
Wacky Chocolate Cake, 148
Waldorf Astoria Cakes, 151

CANDY
Anise Candy, 83
Caramels, 83
Chocolate-Covered
  Cherries, 84
Five-Minute Microwave
  Fudge, 84
Peanut Butter Cups, 85
Peanut Butter
  Marshmallow Fudge, 84
Peanut Clusters, 86
Toffee, 86
Traditional Christmas
  Fudge, 85

CARROTS
Cheesy Carrots, 67
Copper Penny Carrots, 67
Kirsten's Carrots, 67

CHICKEN
Baked Chicken Breasts, 114
Chicken a la Mandy 114
Chicken Enchiladas, 113
Chicken Hot Dish, 113
Chicken Kiev, 112
Chicken Pita Olé, 115
Chicken Stir-Fry, 112
Oodles-o-Noodles Chicken
  Casserole, 111

CHOCOLATE
Bishops Chocolate Pie, 151
Black Bottom Cupcakes, 146
Blonde Brownies, 128
Brownies, 127
Caramel Chocolate
  Squares, 132
Chipper Bars, 132
Chocolate Angel Food
  Cake, 146
Chocolate Ball Cookies, 93
Chocolate Cherry Cake, 147
Chocolate Chip Cake, 147
Chocolate Chip
  Cookies, 136
Chocolate Chip Pudding
  Cookies, 136
Chocolate-Covered
  Cherries, 84
Chocolate Crunch
  Brownies, 129
Chocolate Crunchies, 138
Chocolate Mint Cookies, 94
Chocolate Peanut Butter
  Cookies, 139

Cocoa Brownies, 129
Easy Brownies, 131
Five-Minute Microwave
  Fudge, 84
4-H Brownies, 128
Frosted Crispy Bars, 133
Gold Ribbon Chocolate
  Chip Cookies, 137
Grandma A's Brownies, 130
Grandma Dorothy's
  Chocolate Chip Pie, 153
Ho! Ho! Bars, 135
Malt Brownies, 95
Marble Fudge Bars, 133
Million Dollar Bars, 134
Mint Brownies, 131
Peanut Butter Chocolate
  Squares, 127
Pride-of-Iowa Cookies, 140
Scrumptious Chocolate
  Chip Cookies, 137
Sugar-Free Chocolate
  Peanut Butter Pie, 153
The Great American
  Brownie, 130
Traditional Christmas
  Fudge, 85
Wacky Chocolate
  Cake, 148

COOKIES, BAR
Almond Paste Cookies, 93
Caramel Chocolate
  Squares, 132
Chipper Bars, 132
Frosted Crispy Bars, 133
Ho! Ho! Bars, 135
Marble Fudge Bars, 133
Million Dollar Bars, 134
Oatmeal Toffee Cookies, 95
Peanut Butter Chocolate
  Squares, 127
Take-Along Breakfast
  Bars, 134

COOKIES, BROWNIES
Blonde Brownies, 128
Brownies, 127
Chocolate Crunch
  Brownies, 129
Cocoa Brownies, 129
Easy Brownies, 131
4-H Brownies, 128
Grandma A's Brownies, 130
Malt Brownies, 95
Mint Brownies, 131
The Great American
  Brownie, 130

COOKIES, DROP
Chocolate Chip
  Cookies, 136

Chocolate Chip Pudding
  Cookies, 136
Chocolate Crunchies, 138
Chocolate Peanut Butter
  Cookies, 139
Gold Ribbon Chocolate
  Chip Cookies, 137
Grandpa's Oatmeal-Raisin
  Cookies, 139
Oatmeal Cookies, 140
Pride-of-Iowa Cookies, 140
Pumpkin Cookies, 141
Quick and Easy Peanut
  Butter Cookies, 135
Scrumptious Chocolate
  Chip Cookies, 137

COOKIES, ROLLED
Gingerbread Cutout
  Cookies, 94

COOKIES, SHAPED
Black Bear Molasses Forest
  Cookies, 138
Chocolate Ball Cookies, 93
Chocolate Mint Cookies, 94
Molasses Sugar
  Cookies, 142
Scandinavian Krumkake, 96
Snow on the Mountain, 142
Spritz, 96
Sugar Cookies, 141
Uff-da Queen Kringla, 97

CORN
Cheese Corn, 68
Corn Fritters, 68
Scalloped Corn, 69

CRAFTS, CHILDREN'S
Cinnamon Ornaments, 96
Coal Plant, 91
Play Dough, 89

DESSERTS. *See also* Cakes;
  Cookies, Bar; Cookies,
  Brownies; Cookies,
  Drop; Cookies, Rolled;
  Cookies, Shaped;
  Ice Cream; Pies
Apple Cobbler, 156
Banana Dessert, 157
California Dessert, 157
Cheesecakes, 98
Cream Puff Dessert, 158
Dessert Pizza, 159
Fruit Pizza, 159
Fudge Pudding, 160
Fudge Topping for Ice
  Cream, 162
Microwaved Apple
  Streusel, 156

Index · 169

Peach Crisp, 160
Rhubarb Dessert, 161
Rice Pudding, 160
S'mores-on-a-Grill, 161
Taffy Apple Pizza, 158
Toffee Refrigerator
  Dessert, 162

DESSERTS, LOW-FAT
Anise Candy, 83
Chocolate Angel Food
  Cake, 146
Fudge Topping for Ice
  Cream, 162
Peanut Butter
  Marshmallow Fudge, 84
Rice Pudding, 160
Uff-da Queen Kringla, 97

DIPS
Aletha's Salsa, 77
Bean Dip, 17
Clara's Picante Sauce, 76
Hamburger Dip, 17
Hot Hamburger Dip, 18
Microwave Pork Nachos, 14
Super Nachos, 15

FROSTINGS
Cream Cheese Frosting, 145

GROUND BEEF
Applesauce Meatballs, 103
Baked Spaghetti, 101
Cheeseburger
  Casserole, 104
Ground Beef Pie, 105
Italian Hamburger
  Helper, 105
Lasagna d' Italia, 101
Layered Mexican
  Casserole, 106
Meat Loaf, 102
Mostaccioli, 103
Pizza Hot Dish, 118
Really Good Ravioli, 106
Souper Meat Loaf, 102
Special Hot Chili, 35
Spicy Ground Beef and
  Beans, 104
Taco Casserole, 107
Taco Rice Casserole, 107
Taco Soup, 34
Tater Tot Casserole, 108
Walking Tacos, 92

HOLIDAYS AND SPECIAL OCCASIONS
Almond Paste Cookies, 93
Anise Candy, 83
Birthday Morning
  Cinnamon Rolls, 88

Butterscotch Rolls, 87
Caramels, 83
Cheesecakes, 98
Chocolate Ball
  Cookies, 93
Chocolate-Covered
  Cherries, 84
Chocolate Mint
  Cookies, 94
Christmas T-Braids, 89
Coffee Can Ice Cream, 97
Dutch Almond Torte, 98
Favorite Casserole, 92
Five-Minute Microwave
  Fudge, 84
Gingerbread Cutout
  Cookies, 94
Good-Luck Black-Eyed
  Peas, 69
Heart-Healthy Apple
  Coffee Cake, 90
Holiday French Toast, 91
Malt Brownies, 95
Oatmeal Toffee Cookies, 95
Peanut Butter Cups, 85
Peanut Butter
  Marshmallow Fudge, 84
Peanut Clusters, 86
Pineapple Buns, 90
Scandinavian Krumkake, 96
Spritz, 96
Toffee, 86
Traditional Christmas
  Fudge, 85
Uff-da Queen Kringla, 97
Walking Tacos, 92
Wassail, 87
Zoete Broodges (Dutch
  Sweet Rolls), 91

ICE CREAM
Coffee Can Ice Cream, 97
Vanilla Ice Cream, 161

LAMB
Oriental Lamb Chops, 116

LOW-FAT RECIPES.
  See Beverages, Low-Fat;
  Breads, Low-Fat;
  Desserts, Low-Fat;
  Main Dishes, Low-Fat;
  Salads, Low-Fat;
  Soups, Low-Fat;
  Vegetables, Low-Fat

MAIN DISHES. *See also* Beef;
  Chicken; Ground Beef;
  Lamb; Pasta; Pizza;
  Pork; Salads, Main Dish;
  Seafood; Turkey
Favorite Casserole, 92

Veggie Enchiladas, 120

MAIN DISHES, LOW-FAT
Chicken Pita Olé, 115
Oriental Lamb Chops, 116

MARINADES
Tangy Marinade, 114

PASTA
Baked Spaghetti, 101
Creamy Tuna Casserole, 124
Eighth Street Linguini, 124
Fettuccini and Cheese
  Pie, 123
Fusilli ala Caprese, 78
Italian Hamburger
  Helper, 105
Lasagna d' Italia, 101
Mostaccioli, 103
Oodles-o-Noodles Chicken
  Casserole, 111
Pasta Salad, 41
Pizza Hot Dish, 118
Really Good Ravioli, 106
Vegetable Capellini
  Mascarpone, 80

PIES
Apple Pie, 152
Bishops Chocolate Pie, 151
Classic Pecan Pie, 154
Flaky Pie Pastry, 155
Grandma Dorothy's
  Chocolate Chip
  Pie, 153
Grandma's Pie Pastry, 152
Great-Grandma Betty's
  Custard Pie, 153
Green Tomato Pie, 155
Peanut Butter Pie, 154
Sugar-Free Banana Cream
  Pie, 152
Sugar-Free Chocolate
  Peanut Butter Pie, 153

PIZZA
Homemade Pizza, 117
Jiffy Almond Pan Pizza, 54
Mediterranean Pizzas, 70
Personal Pizzas, 117
Pizza, 118
Pizza Hot Dish, 118
Pizza Potatoes, 72
Pizza Quiche, 119
Upside-Down Pizza, 119

PORK
Favorite Casserole, 92
Glazed Stuffed Chops, 122
Ham Biscuits with Cheese
  Sauce, 120

Hot Ham and Cheese
  Sandwiches, 121
Meat Enchiladas, 121
Pork Chop and Potato
  Scallop, 122
Sweet-and-Sour
  Pork, 123

POTATOES. *See also* Salads,
  Potato
Country Potatoes, 70
801 Maytag Blue Cheese
  Potatoes, 71
Good Potatoes, 71
Party Potatoes, 72
Pizza Potatoes, 72
Potato Refrigerator
  Rolls, 62
Potato Soup, 34
Scalloped Potatoes in a
  Skillet, 71
Twice-Baked Potatoes, 73

SALAD DRESSINGS
Creamy Low-Calorie Salad
  Dressing, 40
Low-Calorie French Salad
  Dressing, 40

SALADS, CONGEALED
Mountain Dew Salad, 37
Peach Salad, 37
Pink Salad, 38
Pretzel Salad, 38
Seven-Layer Gelatin
  Salad, 39
Strawberry Salad, 39

SALADS, FRUIT
Apple Salad, 35
Caramel Apple Salad, 36
Fruit Kabobs, 40
Fruit Salad, 36

SALADS, LOW-FAT
Fruit Kabobs, 40
Fruit Salad, 36
German Potato Salad, 42
Mountain Dew Salad, 37
Seven-Layer Gelatin
  Salad, 39

SALADS, MAIN DISH
Hot Chicken Salad, 44
Pasta Salad, 41
Tasty Taco Salad, 44

SALADS, POTATO
Creamy Potato Salad, 42
German Potato Salad, 42

SALADS, VEGETABLE
Broccoli Delight Salad, 40
Cabbage Salad, 41
Cauliflower Lettuce
  Salad, 41
Gold Coast Salad, 37
Iowa Herbed Tomato
  Salad, 43
Korean Spinach Salad, 43

SEAFOOD
Creamy Tuna Casserole, 124
Eighth Street Linguini, 124

SIDE DISHES
Country Crepes, 76
Fusilli ala Caprese, 78
Homemade Noodles, 75
Ravishing Rice Dish, 78
Rice and Sour Cream
  Casserole, 79
Rice Pilaf, 79
Vegetable Capellini
  Mascarpone, 80
Vegetable Side Dish, 80

SNACKS
Caramel Corn, 21
Caramel Mix, 22
Cashew Mix, 23
Favorite Granola, 21
Flamme Special, 19
Granola Bars, 18
Oyster Cracker Snack, 18
Party Popcorn, 20
Peanut Butter Popcorn, 19
Popcorn Balls, 20
Puppy Chow, 22

SOUPS
Canadian Cheese Soup
  with Popcorn, 32

Cheese Soup, 31
Cheesy Chowder, 30
Cream of Broccoli
  Soup, 32
Dr Pepper Beef Stew, 29
Elephant Stew, 29
Favorite Soup, 33
Football Stew, 30
Four-Onion Soup, 33
Potato Soup, 34
Special Hot Chili, 35
Taco Soup, 34
Vegetable Cheese Soup, 31

SOUPS, LOW-FAT
Favorite Soup, 33
Football Stew, 30

TURKEY
Grilled Turkey Fillets, 115
Mexican Fiesta
  Casserole, 116

VEGETABLES. *See also*
  Individual Kinds
Curried Beans, 65
Favorite Casserole, 92
Good-Luck Black-Eyed
  Peas, 69
Harvard Beets, 65
Mediterranean Pizzas, 70
Sweet Potato Balls, 73
Vegetable Capellini
  Mascarpone, 80
Vegetable Casserole, 74
Vegetable Cheese Soup, 31
Vegetable Side Dish, 80
Veg-et Pockets, 16
Veggie Enchiladas, 120
Zesty Stuffed Tomatoes, 74
Zucchini Rounds, 75

VEGETABLES, LOW-FAT
Curried Beans, 65
Good-Luck Black-Eyed
  Peas, 69
Harvard Beets, 65
Kirsten's Carrots, 67
Veg-et Pockets, 16

Give a Gift That Says "Thank You!"

Every day the Iowa 4-H Foundation supports the development of young people into productive, self-directed, contributing members of society. This happens only through the generous giving of our caring donors.

At the Iowa 4-H Foundation, the best gifts we receive are those that are most meaningful to the donor. That is what makes our honoraria and memorial contributions so special. These one-time gifts are a heartfelt way to recognize someone for their achievements or to remember their lifelong contributions. It's a way to say "thank you" for the positive impact they've had on your life.

To make a gift in the memory or honor of someone, just complete the form below and mail with your check made payable to:

Iowa 4-H Foundation
32 Curtiss Hall, ISU
Ames, Iowa 50011

A Gift to the Iowa 4-H Foundation

❏ In memory of _____

❏ In honor of _____ for
                              Honoree

_____
                Occasion

Given by _____

Address _____

City_____ State_____ Zip_____

Gift amount enclosed $ _____

Send acknowledgement to _____

Address _____

_____ Thank you for caring!

Here's how all the "H's" fit together in the 4-H pledge....

I pledge—

My **Head** to clearer thinking

My **Heart** to greater loyalty

My **Hands** to larger service

My **Health** to better living

For my club, my community, my country and my world.

Alumni Search • 173

The Great 4-H Alumni Search

Can You Help Us?

We try to keep track of our Iowa 4-H members after they leave the program, but it is difficult to stay ahead of all the name and address changes along the way. When we lose contact with our former 4-H'ers, we lose our chance to keep them informed about new programs, special events, and alumni activities. If you were an Iowa 4-H member or know someone who was, please let us know. Just complete the form below and mail to:

Alumni Search
Iowa 4-H Foundation
32 Curtiss Hall, ISU
Ames, Iowa 50011

Name _____

Address _____

City, State, ZIP+4 _____

Phone ( ) _____ ( ) _____
                    Home   Work

E-Mail _____ Fax ( ) _____

❑ Iowa 4-H Alum   ❑ 4-H Alum from another state _____

Years enrolled in 4-H **19** ____ to **19** ____   County _____

Club Name _____

Check the activities or programs in which you participated:

- ❑ 4-H Camp
- ❑ Judging Team
- ❑ 4-H Camp Counselor/Staff
- ❑ State 4-H Officer/Council
- ❑ Campus or Collegiate 4-H
- ❑ National 4-H Congress
- ❑ IFYE
- ❑ NORSKE

- ❑ State Fair
- ❑ State Project Awards
- ❑ Communication Contests
- ❑ State Youth and 4-H Conference
- ❑ Citizenship Washington Focus (CWF)
- ❑ National 4-H Conference
- ❑ LABO

County or state offices held _____

Thank You!

How to join 4-H:

Join the 4-H family!

. . . and justice for all
The Iowa Cooperative Extension Service's programs and policies are consistent with pertinent federal and state laws and regulations on nondiscrimination. Many materials can be made available in alternative formats for ADA clients.

Contact your local county extension office. The helpful staff can tell you all about 4-H.

Order Information • 175

Order Form

Iowa: A Taste of Home
Iowa 4-H Foundation
32 Curtiss Hall, ISU
Ames, Iowa 50011

Make checks payable to: Iowa 4-H Foundation

Name _____

Address _____

City/State/Zip _____

   Please send _____ copies @ $12.00 each $ _____

   Postage and Handling @ $ 2.00 each $ _____

        TOTAL $ _____

Cookbooks may be purchased directly at county Extension offices or at the Iowa 4-H Foundation office.

Order Form

Iowa: A Taste of Home
Iowa 4-H Foundation
32 Curtiss Hall, ISU
Ames, Iowa 50011

Make checks payable to: Iowa 4-H Foundation

Name _____

Address _____

City/State/Zip _____

   Please send _____ copies @ $12.00 each $ _____

   Postage and Handling @ $ 2.00 each $ _____

        TOTAL $ _____

Cookbooks may be purchased directly at county Extension offices or at the Iowa 4-H Foundation office.

4-H is for you! Kids, adults, families, volunteers, and staff are all part of our community.

There is a place for everyone in Iowa 4-H.